WEST VIRGINIA
Hometown Cookbook

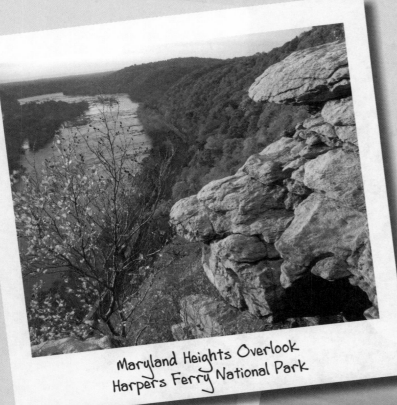

Maryland Heights Overlook
Harpers Ferry National Park

Dolly Sods Wilderness
Monongahela National Forest

WEST VIRGINIA
Hometown Cookbook

BY SHEILA SIMMONS AND KENT WHITAKER

GREAT AMERICAN PUBLISHERS
WWW.GREATAMERICANPUBLISHERS.COM
TOLL-FREE 1.888.854.5954

Great American Publishers

171 Lone Pine Church Road • Lena, MS 39094

TOLL-FREE 1.888.854.5954 • www.GreatAmericanPublishers.com

ISBN 978-1-934817-20-9

10 9 8 7 6 5 4 3 2

by Sheila Simmons & Kent Whitaker

Designed by Roger & Sheila Simmons

Front cover photos: Top Left - Seneca Rocks ©thinkstock/istock/Dwight Nadig • Center - Purple Rhododendron ©thinkstock/istock/Lee Myers • Right - Glade Creek Grist Mill ©thinkstock/istock/Sreedhar Yedlapati • Bottom Food - Apple Butter Bread ©James Stefuik

Back cover: Food - Trout Amandine - James Stefuik • Stewie the Hot Dog ©Stewart's Original Hot Dogs

Inside photos: p1 In State Shape ©thinkstock/istock/Teresa Yeager • p2 Maryland Heights ©thinkstock/istock/Richard Gunion; Dolly Sods ©thinkstock/istock/EJ-J • p9 Pepperoni Rolls ©Kent Whitaker • p14 Hummus ©thinkstock/istock/Natasha • p11 Pumpkin Dip ©thinkstock/istock/MariaShumova • p16 Black Bean & Corn Salsa ©thinkstock/istock/Jack Puccio • p19 Garlic Mustard Pesto ©Gwen Balogh • p23 Wassail ©thinkstock/istock/tacar • p24 Smoothie ©thinkstock/istock/HandmadePictures • p27 Cornbread ©thinkstock/istock/MSPhotographicCollection • p30 Butterhorns ©thinkstock/istock/Metkalova • p35 Apple Butter Bread ©James Stefuik • p37 Blueberry Corn Muffins ©thinkstock/istock/letterberry • p38 Apple Butter ©thinkstock/istock/Laura Flugga • p45 Zucchini Pancakes ©thinkstock/istock/YelenaYemchuk • p55 Prison Museum ©thinkstock/istock/NoDerog • p56 Chicken & Rice Soup ©thinkstock/istock/paulbinet • p59 Squash soup ©thinkstock/istock/ginauf • p65 Soups Chapter ©thinkstock/istock/OlgaMiltsovaCollection • p66 Blackwater Falls ©thinkstock/istock/John_Brueske • p69 Pea Salad ©thinkstock/istock/Hemera/Jaimie Duplass • p70 Coleslaw ©thinkstock/istock/bhofack2 • p72 Broccoli Salad ©thinkstock/istock/Donna Moulton • p75 Blue Cheese Dressing ©thinkstock/istock/StephanieFrey • p85 Squash Casserole ©thinkstock/istock/Andrea Skjold • p79 Vegetables Chapter ©thinkstock/istock/cartela • p80 Whitewater raftng ©thinkstock/istock/Andrea Pelletier • p91 Cauliflower ©thinkstock/istock/Sarsmis • p94 Honey ©Nick Durm • p97 Beef Chapter ©thinkstock/istock/LeeAnnWhite • p105 Hot Dog Sauce ©thinkstock/istock/sheldrake • p108 Bear Rocks ©thinkstock/istock/JNevitt • p110 Pork Chops ©thinkstock/istock/soponbiz • p116 River ©thinkstock/istock/Sreedhar Yedlapati • p126 Tamarack, photo courtesy of Tamarack The Best of West Virginia • p129 Chicken Chapter ©thinkstock/istock/adlifemarketing • p132 Chicken Cacciatore ©thinkstock/istock/Joe Gough • p138 Spicy Almond Chicken ©thinkstock/istock/Elena Gaak • p143 Honey Chicken Wings ©thinkstock/istock/rez-art • p149 Fish Chapter ©James Stefuik • p156 Baked Fish ©thinkstock/Purestock • p161 Bridge ©thinkstock/istock/Nicholas Krayer • p164 Honey Grilled Fish ©thinkstock/istock/deymos • p167 Shrimp Boil ©thinkstock/istock/Danny Hooks • p169 Cake Chapter ©thinkstock/istock/Jack Puccio • p177 Hummingbird Cake ©thinkstock/istock/Aiselin82 • p179 Chocolate Cake ©thinkstock/istock/Matt Brennan • p183 Covered Bridge ©thinkstock/istock/John_Brueske • p185 Carrot Cake ©thinkstock/istock/ LeventKonuk • p186 Blackberry Cake ©thinkstock/istock/ Lesyy • p189 Pumpkin Cupcakes ©thinkstock/istock/StephanieFrey • p190 Butternut Pound Cake ©thinkstock/istock/fotogal • p193 Cookies Chapter ©thinkstock/istock/StephanieFreyCollection • p194 Apple Butter Bars ©thinkstock/istock/ Lilechka75 • p196 Kelly points edible plant ©Alan Balogh • p196 Identifying Plants ©Warren Balogh • p196 Jerusalem Artichoke ©Warren Balogh • p198 Peanut Butter Oatmeal ©thinkstock/istock/Ron Orman Jr • p200 Making molasses ©Calhoun Chronicle Newspaper - Bill Bailey • p203 Truffles ©thinkstock/istock/eyewave • p208 Fudge ©thinkstock/istock/violleta • p213 Cabin ©thinkstock/istock/Chitra Tatachar • p217 Pies Chapter ©thinkstock/istock/Justine GecewiczCollection • p220 Apple Butter Pumpkin Pie ©thinkstock/istock/chas53 • p230 Baklava ©thinkstock/istock/gojak • p236 Rafting ©thinkstock/istock/imagegrafx • p239 mountain ©thinkstock/istock/John_Brueske Keywords • p241 Index Chapter ©thinkstock/istock/EJ-J • p247 church ©thinkstock/istock/Sreedhar Yedlapati • p252 photo courtesy of West Virginia Maple Syrup Festival

WEST VIRGINIA

CONTENTS

INTRODUCTION

Several years ago Sheila and I teamed up to pen the STATE HOMETOWN COOKBOOK SERIES. It would be the first cookbook series for Great American Publishers founded by Sheila and her husband Roger. Since then the series has grown to include editions for Tennessee, Georgia, South Carolina, Mississippi, Texas, Louisiana, and now West Virginia.

If there's one thing we've learned along the way, it is that every state is not the same when it comes to food. And yet, in some ways, they are all similar. Each state has a reputation for a certain type of food and/or ethnic dishes, and at the same time, each state has a firm grip on hometown cooking, family favorites, traditions, and of course classic comfort foods. Each state's heritage creates one slice in the pie of our nation's culinary history.

My wife Allyson and I are always amazed at the range of dishes we discover when researching a state for the series, as well as the hospitality of the people we meet along the way. West Virginia is no different. Not all pepperoni rolls and wild ramps, this fascinating state offers many culinary delights from **Blueberry Corn Muffins with Lemon Sauce** to **West Virginia Honey Mustard Chicken Pie**, from **Hillbilly Hot Dog Sauce** to **Orange Juice Taffy**. And, if you are looking for pepperoni rolls and wild ramps, you'll find that too. Check out **Pepperoni Roll Poppers** and **Ramp-Wrapped Chicken Breasts**.

The slow food and local food movements have chefs and cooks looking to the past for inspiration. You will find the food heritage in West Virginia has an amazing lineage. From **Leather Britches** to **Depression Raisin Cake**, **Nelson Family Bread Pudding** to **Moonshiner Grilling Sauce** (from a verified moonshiner), you will discover recipes that have been handed down for generations.

The STATE HOMETOWN COOKBOOK SERIES was born of a desire to save our culinary history, one dish at a time. This West Virginia edition lives up to that goal with recipes from cooks both old and new. The sort of recipes you will want to hand-down to your own family for many years to come. Your children and their children and their children will all enjoy delicious recipes like **West Virginia Cast-Iron Sugar Snap Peas**, **My Mama's Meatloaf**, and **West Virginia Hornets Nest Cake**. From dipping cookies and pretzels in melted chocolate at Christmas, to learning to cook your grandmother's hash brown casserole, to hand-picking ramps, drying beans, home canning vegetables . . . or eating a pepperoni roll, time spent in the kitchen with family is valuable.

When it comes to West Virginia, family memories wouldn't be complete without Apple Butter and this cookbook has you covered . . . from **Apple Butter Cake** to **Apple Butter Bars** to **Apple Butter Pumpkin Pie**. Interested in making your own Apple Butter from scratch? You'll find versions for the slow cooker, microwave and stovetop. There is even an **Oven-Baked Apple Butter** recipe in the book—a distinctly delicious taste of the Mountain State.

As always, this book wouldn't be possible without the help of many people. Our sincerest thank you goes to the people of West Virginia who shared their recipes, their stories and information about their food festivals . . . always with patience and sincerity. Thank you to our Great American team supporting our efforts—Brooke Craig, Director of Operations, who knows how to make things happen, Diane Rothery for keeping us all together, Pam Johnson for organizing, researching, and generally keeping things on track, Cyndi Clark for her beautiful designs, Pam Larson and our sales team supreme—Krista Griffin, Tory Hackett, Amber Feiok, Anita Musgrove, and Christy Kent, thank you all for your endless hard work. As with previous books in the series, we dedicate *West Virginia Hometown Cookbook* to our spouses, Allyson Whitaker and Roger Simmons, as well as our children, Macee Whitaker, as well as Nicholas Williams and Ryan and Shelbie Williams, plus our family and friends both of old and those we met along the way on this journey of preserving each state's culinary heritage.

If you are ready for a wonderfully down-home and delicious taste of West Virginia, dive right in.

Happy Cooking

Kent Whitaker & Sheila Simmons

"Whatever you do, work at it with all your heart, as work-ing for the Lord, not for human masters, since you know that you will receive an inheritance from the Lord as a reward. It is the Lord Christ you are serving."

Colossians 3:23-24 (NIV)

APPETIZERS & BEVERAGES

Pepperoni Roll Poppers,
page 18

Tailgate Spinach Dip

1 (10-ounce) package frozen chopped
    spinach
2 cups mayonnaise
¼ cup finely chopped onion
Several drops Texas Pete hot sauce
2 tablespoons freeze-dried chives

*Janet Whitten of Nimitz
gave me this recipe
for my West Virginia
Mountaineer football
page. It's almost too easy
to be this delicious.*

Cook spinach and drain very well. Add remaining ingredients and mix thoroughly. Chill before serving; best if made the night before. Serve with favorite crackers or veggies.

Larry Meador, Hinton, www.tailgatewvu.com

ThistleDew Farm Honey Dip

½ cup ketchup
¼ cup honey
2 tablespoons lemon juice

1 teaspoon cornstarch
½ teaspoon garlic salt

Combine all ingredients in a microwave-safe bowl. Microwave on high (100% power) 30 seconds at a time, stirring each time, for 2 to 3 minutes or until mixture boils and thickens. Cool. Serve as a dip for chicken nuggets and/or vegetables.

Steve & Ellie Conlon, ThistleDew Farm, Proctor

Pumpkin Dip with Graham Crackers

Looking for a great after school snack or light dessert? Try this dip served with graham crackers or graham sticks.

1 (30-ounce) can pumpkin purée
1 (8-ounce) carton Cool Whip, light or fat free
1 (5.1-ounce) box instant vanilla pudding or instant pumpkin pie pudding
1 teaspoon pumpkin pie spice

Mix all ingredients together and serve with graham crackers or graham sticks. Makes 5 to 6 cups.

Heather Rice, RD LD,
Marshall University
Nutrition Education Program,
Huntington

Cheese Ball Dip

2 (8-ounce) packages Greek cream
   cheese, softened
1 (15-ounce) can crushed pineapple,
   drained
3 green onions, chopped
1 (3-ounce) package chipped beef,
   chopped
¼ teaspoon Lawry's seasoned salt,
   optional

Whip cream cheese until light and fluffy.
Add remaining ingredients; mix well. Place
mixture in an 8x8-inch pan and chill. Serve
1 tablespoon in a soufflé cup with 2 Triscuits
on the side. Makes about 45 servings.

Marshall University
Nutrition Education Program,
Huntington

PHOTOS COURTESY OF VISIT SOUTHERN WV

Kirkwood Winery Grape Stomping Wine Festival

Summersville
Third Weekend in September

For more than 20 years, the Kirkwood Winery Grape
Stomping Wine Festival has provided fun for the
whole family. This unique festival features live music,
dance groups, handmade crafts, and good food.
Popular music groups perform each year; check
the website for the full line-up. Everyone loves the
Grape Stomping and Grape Eating Contests. Enjoy a
free glass with admission to the wine tasting.

304-872-7332 • www.kirkwood-wine.com

Bacon Cheese Ball Bites

2 (8-ounce) packages cream cheese, softened
2 cups shredded sharp Cheddar cheese
4 ounces Roquefort cheese, crumbled
1 (3-ounce) package bacon bits
1 small onion, grated
¼ teaspoon Worcestershire sauce
¼ teaspoon garlic salt

Combine all ingredients, mixing well with hands. Shape into ¾-inch round balls and place on a cookie sheet lined with wax paper or in miniature muffin cups. Refrigerate at least 1 hour. Remove from refrigerator about 15 minutes before serving. Place on tray and serve with crackers. Makes about 24.

Blue Smoke Salsa Cheese Ball

Since founding Blue Smoke Salsa, I've been trying different recipes using my salsa as an ingredient. This cheese ball recipe could not be simpler, and it's delicious, too.

2 (8-ounce) packages cream cheese, softened
1 (8-ounce) package shredded Cheddar cheese
8 ounces (½ jar) Blue Smoke Salsa, any heat

Mix all ingredients together and form into a ball. If desired, roll in pecans (crushed or whole). Wrap in plastic wrap and chill about a half hour or longer to really let the flavors meld. Serve with crackers.

Robin Hildebrand, President and Founder,
Blue Smoke Salsa, Ansted

Extra Easy Hummus

1 (15.5-ounce) can garbanzo
   beans
1 clove garlic, crushed

2 teaspoons ground cumin
½ teaspoon salt
1 tablespoon olive oil

Drain beans, reserving juice. In blender or food processor, mix beans until smooth. Add garlic, cumin, salt and olive oil. Blend together. If hummus is too thick, stir in reserved juice to desired consistency.

West Virginia University Extension Service,
Morgantown, www.ext.wvu.edu

Book Club Salsa

12 ounces tomatoes, diced
1 medium red onion, diced
1 handful chopped fresh cilantro
Juice of 1 lemon
2 tablespoons white vinegar
1 clove garlic
3 to 5 serrano peppers, diced
Salt and pepper

Combine everything except salt and pepper in a food processer and pulse until incorporated but still chunky. Add salt and pepper to taste.

Chad Wood, Bradley

My wife hosts a book club the last Friday of every month. It's one of my favorite evenings—despite the fact that I don't read the book. It's an occasion that calls for a lot of cooking and that's what I like. The club members always enjoy this salsa served with chips for dipping.

Black-Eyed Joe's Salsa

1 (28-ounce) can whole unseasoned
    tomatoes
Juice of 2 limes
½ red onion, chopped
1 clove garlic, chopped
1 jalapeño pepper, seeded and
    chopped
1 serrano pepper, seeded and
    chopped

½ bunch cilantro, chopped
1 teaspoon sugar
1 tablespoon honey
½ tablespoon olive oil
¼ teaspoon cumin
¼ teaspoon kosher salt
¼ teaspoon fresh ground black pepper

This recipe from Joe Bryant is so good it was an instant hit on my tailgate menu and on my webpage about West Virginia Mountaineer Football.

Place everything into a food processor or blender and chop to desired consistency.

Larry Meador, Hinton, www.tailgatewvu.com

Black Bean & Corn Salsa

1 (15-ounce) can black beans, rinsed
1 (15-ounce) can whole-kernel corn, drained
2 tomatoes, finely chopped
3 green onions, finely chopped
½ green bell pepper, finely chopped
½ red bell pepper, finely chopped
½ yellow bell pepper, finely chopped
¼ cup red wine vinegar
¼ cup olive oil
½ teaspoon white pepper
¾ teaspoon salt
1 tablespoon Tabasco hot sauce, optional
1 teaspoon cumin, optional

Combine black beans and corn with finely chopped vegetables. Add vinegar, oil and seasonings; mix well. Refrigerate and marinate overnight. Serve with Scoops corn chips or simply eat as it is. Enjoy!

Marshall University Nutrition Education Program, Huntington

Easy Black Bean Salsa

2 (15-ounce) cans seasoned black beans, drained
3 fresh tomatoes, diced or 2 (14.5-ounce) cans petite diced tomatoes
½ purple onion, finely chopped
1 large Vidalia onion, finely chopped
1 jalapeño pepper, seeded and finely chopped
2 cloves garlic, finely chopped
Juice of 2 limes
Sea or kosher salt
Cholula hot sauce to taste
Chopped cilantro to taste

Combine all ingredients except salt, hot sauce and cilantro. Mix well. Add 1 tablespoon salt, dashes of hot sauce and a generous amount of chopped cilantro. Taste and adjust seasonings to taste. Cover and chill before serving with chips of your choice.

Pryce M. Haynes III, Huntington

Spicy Tortilla Roll-Ups

1 (8-ounce) package fat-free cream cheese, softened
1 (9-ounce) package frozen spinach, cooked and well drained
1 any color bell pepper, chopped very fine or 1 teaspoon curry powder (not both)
¼ cup fat-free mayonnaise
10 burrito-size flour tortillas

Mix cream cheese, spinach, bell pepper and mayonnaise. Spread on flour tortillas. Roll up and chill. Cut into bite-size pieces or serve whole instead of a sandwich.

West Virginia University Extension Service, Morgantown, www.ext.wvu.edu

Pepperoni Roll Poppers

1 (7.5-ounce) can rolled biscuits (not the flaky kind)
1 (6-ounce) package sliced pepperoni
Sliced provolone cheese to taste
Italian seasoning to taste

Cut each biscuit in half and flatten. Center a few pepperoni pieces and a small amount of cheese in the middle (not too much cheese or you'll have a mess). Sprinkle with Italian seasoning and roll up. Pinch edges to keep it from unrolling, but don't worry about closing completely. Place on cookie sheet and bake at 375° until golden brown, about 20 minutes.

Hannah B. Turner

Bacon and Swiss Deviled Eggs

1 dozen hard-cooked eggs
½ cup cooked crumbled bacon
¼ cup mayonnaise
2½ tablespoons apple cider vinegar
2 teaspoons sugar
2 teaspoons honey mustard
½ cup finely shredded Swiss cheese
Salt and pepper to taste
Green onions, finely chopped, for garnish

Shell eggs and cut in half lengthwise. Remove yolks and mash until smooth. Add remaining ingredients, except green onions, and stir until well blended. Spoon or pipe yolk mixture into egg whites. Garnish with green onions.

Garlic Mustard Pesto with Black Walnuts

3 cups garlic mustard leaves*,
    washed, patted dry, and packed
1 dozen or so wild ramps green
    leaves, about 6 inches long,
    blanched 30 seconds, then placed
    in ice cold water and patted dry
2 garlic cloves, peeled and chopped
1 cup black walnuts, toasted in oven
    or toaster oven at 350° about 10
    minutes
1 cup olive oil
½ teaspoon lemon juice (to help keep
    the fresh green color)
1 cup grated Parmesan cheese

Combine garlic mustard leaves, wild ramp leaves, garlic and walnuts in food processor and process. With motor running, add olive oil slowly. Add lemon juice. Shut off motor. Add cheese and process briefly to combine. Serve warm over pasta, or spread on crackers, crusty bread or warm flatbread wedges. It makes a great topping for baked fish. Keeps about a week in fridge in covered container. Freezes well.

*Note: For the garlic mustard leaves, use the young, more triangular leaves (when the plant just begins to bolt) as they are less bitter than the older, rounded leaves at the base of the plant. Leaf stems are okay.

Wild Edibles Festival

Grilled Fruit Kabobs with Midori Coconut Reduction

1 cup Midori, reduced in saucepan by half
2 tablespoons honey
4 (10-inch) bamboo skewers
¼ fresh pineapple, cored and cut into 8 (1-inch) cubes
1 banana, peeled and cut into 8 portions
1 Gala, Fuji or Red Delicious apple, cored and cut into 8 (1-inch) cubes
2 medium-size fresh peaches cut into 1-inch chunks
½ cup toasted coconut

Soak skewers in water 1 hour. Combine Midori and honey in a small bowl; set aside. Thread each skewer with a slice of each fruit. Repeat in the same sequence. Preheat grill to medium high. Place kabobs on grill and cook until lightly caramelized, about 3 minutes each side, brushing with Midori and honey mixture. Remove kabobs from grill; garnish with coconut and serve immediately.

*Tamarack: The Best of West Virginia, Beckley,
www.tamarackwv.com*

Strawberry & Orange Summer Icee

2 cups chopped strawberries
1 orange or 2 tangerines, peeled
2 (1-gram) packages Stevia (or preferred sugar substitute)
2 (.11-ounce) packages wild strawberry flavoring for bottled water
1 cup water
Ice

Process everything in a blender until smooth. (If your blender is like the one we used when we first starting make this, add the ice and water first to fully crush then add remaining ingredients.)

C.L. Feinstein, WVU

Lemonade Festival

Bluefield • Last Weekend in August

Bluefield Preservation Society hosts the Lemonade Festival in the Depot District the last weekend of August. The celebration of The Greater Bluefield Chamber of Commerce's long-standing lemonade promotion features: art exhibits, parade, antique car show, food court, arts and crafts, LemonMade Cook-Off, lemonade promotion display, lemon hunt, family fun park, musical acts from acclaimed gospel groups to local artists, with a grand finale act in the historic Granada Theater. The GBCC's lemonade promotion began in 1939. Arguably the most unique and highly recognized tradition celebrated in the Bluefields, the lemonade promotion is well loved by citizens and has gained national exposure.

304-589-0239
www.bluefieldpreservationsociety.com

Blueberry Mint Lemonade

2 cups fresh-squeezed lemon juice
¾ cup fine sugar
4 cups water
½ cup blueberries
Mint leaves, garnish
Lemon slices, garnish

Combine lemon juice, sugar and water in a pitcher; mix well. When ready to serve, fill 4 tall glasses with ice. Add ⅛ cup blueberries to each glass. Fill with lemonade and garnish each glass with mint leaves and a slice of lemon.

Lemonade Festival

West Virginia Iced Apple Cider Punch

Mom would always make this in fall and winter, especially for Thanksgiving and Christmas. Make it an adult beverage with champagne or without alcohol using sparkling white grape juice. Either way, it's delicious.

6 to 7 cups apple cider
2 to 3 cups orange juice
½ cup lemon juice
1 (25.4-ounce) bottle sparkling white grape juice or 1 bottle champagne

Combine ingredients in a punch bowl; mix well. Add ice and serve immediately.

Barney Gullatt, West Virginia Mountaineers

West Virginia Hot Apple Cider Punch

1 gallon apple cider
1 cup brown sugar
2 teaspoons allspice
2 teaspoons cloves
½ teaspoon salt
2 dashes ground nutmeg
4 large cinnamon sticks

This is Mom's punch recipe. For an adult version, add ¼ cup regular or cinnamon-flavored bourbon.

Combine all ingredients in a slow cooker set to medium. Turn to low when heated. Serve hot.

Barney Gullatt, West Virginia Mountaineers

Wassail dates back to old England when it was made to celebrate a good harvest. The spices in this recipe make it great for cool weather.

Golden Delicious Wassail

1 gallon apple cider from West Virginia
    Golden Delicious apples
1 cup cranberry juice
2 oranges
2 to 3 whole cinnamon sticks
6 to 8 whole cloves
1 teaspoon nutmeg
1 teaspoon ginger

Combine cider in a large pot with cranberry juice. Slice oranges in half and squeeze juice directly into pot. After squeezing, slice oranges into 3 or 4 pieces and place in pot. Add cinnamon sticks and spices. Cook over high heat about 5 minutes. Reduce heat to low, cover and cook 2 hours or longer. Strain before serving. Garnish each cup with half a fresh orange slice and/or a cinnamon stick.

Barney Gullatt,
West Virginia Mountaineers

Tropical Honey Bloom Smoothie

1½ cups low-fat milk
2 ripe medium bananas,
   peeled
¼ cup honey
1 cup plain or vanilla yogurt

1 teaspoon vanilla (omit if
   using vanilla yogurt)
½ teaspoon ground cinnamon
Dash ground nutmeg
5 or more ice cubes

Combine milk, bananas, honey, yogurt, vanilla, cinnamon and nutmeg in blender; process until thick and creamy. Add ice cubes, 1 at a time, and blend until smooth.

Steve & Ellie Conlon, ThistleDew Farm, Proctor

BREAD & BREAKFAST

Tried and True
Cornbread, page 27

Native American Chestnut Cornbread

6 corn blades (leaves), washed and
    scalded in boiling water
1 cup plain ground cornmeal
1 cup coarsely ground cornmeal
    (such as yellow corn grits)
¼ teaspoon salt
¼ teaspoon baking soda
½ cup sugar
2 cups hulled, peeled and chopped
    chestnuts
1 cup water

Native Americans of the Appalachian Mountains enjoy this bread made from a recipe handed down through the generations. Chinese or European chestnuts often are substituted, but if you can find American chestnuts, use a bit less sugar as the American chestnuts are naturally sweet.

Shred 1 corn blade from end to end to create narrow, 1-inch-wide strips. To make bread dough, mix cornmeal, salt, soda and sugar. (Use of yellow corn grits will add texture to the cooked bread.) Add chestnuts. Add water slowly to make stiff bread dough; the full cup may not be needed. Place a portion of dough on the wide end of a whole corn blade. Wrap leaf around mixture, first sides and then large end, molding dough into a rectangular shape about 2 inches wide, 4 inches long, and 1 inch thick. Be sure dough is completely covered by leaf. Leave narrow end of corn blade free and unwrapped for the next step.

Split narrow end of corn blade into 2 strands and wrap each strand in opposite directions around the rest of the wrapped bundle. Tie the 2 strands into a knot to securely bind chestnut cornmeal mixture within leaf wrapping. Tie with additional 1 inch strips (from first step, above) if necessary. Gently drop wrapped packets in boiling water and simmer 60 minutes. After boiling, remove packets, drain and cool. Unwrap packets while still warm and serve with butter. Leftover bread can be reheated in a skillet and served warm with butter.

Doug Gillis, West Virginia Chestnut Festival

Tried and True Cornbread

3 tablespoons shortening
2 cups stone-ground cornmeal
2 pinches baking soda
1 tablespoon sugar
1 cup flour
3 teaspoons baking powder
1 teaspoon salt
1½ cups buttermilk
1 egg, lightly beaten

Richard and Jane Milam of St. Albans share this cornbread recipe which is similar to one Grandma Ethel Nelson used when they'd visit the homeplace on Witcher Creek.

Preheat oven to 500°. Before mixing bread, put shortening into iron skillet, place it in hot oven to season being careful not to burn the shortening. Remove skillet just before time to pour in cornbread mixture. Mix dry ingredients together, make a well in the center and add buttermilk and egg. Stir slowly until batter is smooth. Do not beat or over mix. If too dry, add a little water. Pour into heated skillet and bake 20 minutes. The cornbread should turn out crusty on the outside, moist and done on the inside—just the way it's been in the mountains of West Virginia for years.

Richard and Jane Milam,
St. Albans Historical Society, St. Albans

Hillbilly Biscuits

¾ cup shortening
5 cups flour
1 teaspoon salt
1 tablespoon sugar
1 teaspoon baking soda

3 teaspoons baking powder
1 (.25-ounce) package yeast
½ cup warm water
2 cups buttermilk

Cut shortening into flour. Add dry ingredients except yeast and mix. Dissolve yeast in warm water and mix into the dry ingredients. Add buttermilk and mix well. Cover and store in cool, dry place. Bake as needed by shaping into biscuits and baking at 425° until brown.

Mom's Sausage Biscuits

½ pound ground bulk sausage
2 cups sifted all-purpose flour
4 teaspoons baking powder
½ teaspoon salt
½ teaspoon cream of tartar
2 teaspoons sugar
½ cup shortening or margarine
⅔ cup milk
½ cup grated Parmesan cheese

This recipe, from my mother Norma Cotton's recipe collection, was a standard almost every weekend, especially on a wintery Sunday morning. Some prefer the biscuits plain, or with butter or honey on top.

Brown sausage, drain and set aside. Preheat oven to 450°. Mix flour, baking powder, salt, cream of tartar and sugar together. Work in shortening with a pastry blender until mixture resembles coarse crumbs. Stir in milk all at once. Add sausage and Parmesan cheese. Drop by spoonfuls onto an ungreased baking sheet and bake 10 to 12 minutes.

Steve Cotton, Voice of the Thundering Herd,
Marshall University, Huntington

Basic Baking Mix

8 cups all-purpose flour
⅓ cup baking powder
2 teaspoons salt

8 teaspoons sugar, optional
1 cup shortening

Mix dry ingredients together. Using a pastry blender or fork, cut in shortening until it creates a coarse texture. Store in a tightly sealed container in the pantry if using soon or in the refrigerator, where it lasts longer.

To make biscuits, add ⅓ cup milk to each cup dry mix. Shape and bake at 450° for 12 to 15 minutes.

For pancakes, add enough milk to get the pancake-batter consistency you want.

Mary Jones, Kenna

Yummy Breakfast Rolls

2 (8-ounce) tubes crescent rolls
2 (8-ounce) packages cream
  cheese, softened
1 teaspoon vanilla extract

1¼ cups sugar, divided
½ cup margarine, melted
1 teaspoon cinnamon

Unroll 1 can crescent rolls into bottom of a 9x13-inch pan. (Do not press seams together.) Mix cream cheese with vanilla and 1 cup sugar; spread over rolls. Place second can of rolls over top. Top with melted margarine. Combine remaining ¼ cup sugar with cinnamon; sprinkle over top. Bake 30 minutes at 350°.

Bill Lilly, Lilly and Line Families, Jumping Branch

Grandma Cotton's Butterhorns

The kitchen at Grandma and Grandpa Cotton's house always smelled like flour because of the baking Grandma did. She even painted her most-used recipes on the kitchen cupboard doors. This recipe originated in Northern Michigan where I grew up but is now part of my family's West Virginia recipe collection. Baking time will vary depending on the size of your butterhorns.

1 cup scalded milk
½ cup butter, cut into pieces plus more for
    tops of horns
3 eggs
½ cup sugar
1 teaspoon salt
1 (.25-ounce) package quick dry yeast
4½ cups bread flour
Sugar for sprinkling

Cool scalded milk by adding butter and set aside. Beat eggs and add sugar. Add salt. Add yeast to cooled milk and butter. Add yeast mixture to egg mixture. Add flour. Knead and form into 3 equal balls. Roll them around in a greased bowl so they will stay separate. Let rise until very light. Roll or pat balls into ½-inch thick circles. Spread circles with butter and cut each circle into 8 to 12 pie-shaped wedges. Roll each wedge from base to point. Place on greased cookie sheet with point tucked under. Sprinkle with sugar. Bake at 375° on top rack until lightly browned, 20 to 25 minutes.

Steve Cotton, Voice of the Thundering Herd,
Marshall University, Huntington

John's Favorite Herb Bread

1¼ cups warm water
1 (.25-ounce) package active dry yeast
2 tablespoons sugar
2 tablespoons soft shortening or
    1 tablespoon each unsweetened
    applesauce and vegetable oil
1 tablespoon caraway seeds
¾ teaspoon nutmeg
1 teaspoon crumbled dried sage or 1
    tablespoon minced fresh
1 teaspoon parsley flakes or
    1 tablespoon minced fresh
3 cups all-purpose flour, divided

The Gillum House, purchased by Troy and Anna Brane Gillum in 1918, dates back to 1912. The Gillums were deeply involved in their community as are the current owners. Kathleen Moran Panek, proud proprietor of the bed and breakfast, says that this is one of her husband's favorite recipes.

Put warm water in a medium bowl and sprinkle yeast and sugar on top. Let it sit 5 minutes. Add shortening, herbs and half the flour. Beat with a spoon or use a mixer on medium speed for 2 minutes. Add remaining flour and mix with a spoon. Cover with a clean cloth and let rise in a warm place until double in bulk, about 30 minutes. Stir batter down by beating with a spoon, about 25 strokes. Spread evenly in a 9x5-inch bread pan sprayed with nonstick spray. Smooth top with floured hand. Cover and let rise 30 to 40 minutes. Preheat oven to 375°. Bake 45 to 50 minutes or until browned. Remove from pan immediately and cool on a rack. This recipe can be doubled or tripled.

Kathleen Moran Panek,
Gillum House Bed & Breakfast, Shinnston

Sourdough Starter

DAY 1:

Mix ⅓ cup flour and ¼ cup water in a glass bowl until flour is fully hydrated. Mixture will be thick and glue-like in consistency. Cover loosely with plastic wrap, set it in a warm spot and let it rest for 24 hours.

DAY 2:

Your starter will still look like glue and there may be bubbles forming but it will not have grown much in size. Mix in ¼ cup flour and ⅛ cup room temperature water. Stir well and cover loosely with plastic wrap.

DAY 3:

Your starter should now be double in size and you should notice a smell. Even if it smells terrible, it's okay. The smell should go away. Stir your starter and look for spider web-like strings—this is a good sign. If the surface is dry and crusty, break it up and stir it back in. Once you have stirred it up, throw away half of it and add ¼ cup flour and ⅛ cup room temperature water. Mix completely and cover again.

DAY 4:

If your mixture is bubbly and has a pleasant, sour smell it is ready to use. If your starter should ever develop a pink, orange or other strange-colored tint to it THROW IT OUT IMMEDIATELY and start over. After day 4, your starter can be stored in the refrigerator (covered) until ready to use. When using your starter, always replenish with equal amounts of flour and water, i.e., if you use 1 cup of starter, replace with 1 cup flour and 1 cup water. Leave the starter at room temperature until bubbly again, then refrigerate.

Mary Jones, Kenna

Tabler Family Date Bread

Dave Tabler, an historian of Appalachian life, has deep family roots in West Virginia. This recipe, given to Dave's Mother, shows how home cooking and handwritten recipes passed down through generations help preserve a slice of family and culinary history. He remembers this recipe's original author being one of those cooks who worked from memory, using "a pinch of this" and "a bit of that." Handwritten recipes are filled with life!

1 stick margarine or ¼ cup oil
2 eggs, slightly beaten
1 cup chopped dates
1 cup chopped raisins
1 cup chopped apple
2 cups whole-wheat flour or
    white flour
1 cup quick oats
1 tablespoon baking soda
¼ teaspoon salt
½ cup honey, optional
1 cup sour milk (1 cup milk with
    1 tablespoon vinegar; set aside
    5 minutes)
Chopped nuts, optional

In a bowl, cream margarine; add eggs, dates, raisins and apple. Mix dry ingredients together and stir into margarine mixture. Add remaining ingredients. Spoon into a greased and floured loaf pan and bake at 325° about 45 minutes or until toothpick comes out clean.

Dave Tabler and Family, Martinsburg

Carrot Bread

8 medium carrots, divided
1⅓ cups unbleached all-purpose
  flour
1 teaspoon baking soda
¼ teaspoon baking powder
¾ teaspoon kosher salt
1 cup sugar

6 tablespoons (¾ stick) unsalted
  butter, softened
2 large eggs
⅓ cup buttermilk or ⅓ cup whole
  milk mixed with ½ teaspoon
  lemon juice

Preheat oven to 350°. Grease the bottom and sides of an 8½-inch loaf pan with nonstick cooking spray or butter. Peel and slice 3 carrots into ¼-inch rounds. Bring a medium saucepan of salted water to a boil, add the sliced carrots and cook until soft, about 10 minutes. Drain. Let cool and then purée in a food processor or blender. Coarsely grate the remaining 5 carrots (you should have 2 cups). Set both the puréed carrots and grated carrots aside.

Mix flour, baking soda, baking powder and salt in a bowl. In a separate medium bowl, use a stiff spoon to mix sugar and butter until smooth. Stir in eggs, 1 at a time, until combined. Stir in buttermilk, carrot puree and grated carrots. Add flour mixture and mix until well blended. Spread batter in prepared pan. Bake until a bamboo skewer or toothpick inserted in the middle comes out clean, about 55 to 65 minutes. Remove from oven and cool 15 minutes. Run a small knife around bread to loosen it from pan, and then turn it out onto a cutting board or plate. Cool completely before cutting into slices. Bread will keep at room temperature, wrapped in plastic, 4 days or frozen for 2 months.

Mary Jones, Kenna

Apple Butter Bread

1½ cups all-purpose flour
¾ teaspoon baking soda
½ teaspoon baking powder
½ teaspoon salt
½ teaspoon ground nutmeg
¼ teaspoon ground cloves

⅓ cup butter, softened
1 cup sugar
1 egg, beaten
1¼ cups apple butter
½ cup chopped walnuts (optional)

Preheat oven to 350°. Grease a 9-inch loaf pan. Mix flour, baking soda, baking powder, salt, nutmeg and cloves in a bowl. In a separate large bowl, beat butter and sugar with an electric mixer until smooth. Add egg and apple butter; continue beating until smooth. Mix in flour mixture until just incorporated. Fold in walnuts and mix by hand just until incorporated. Pour into prepared loaf pan. Bake 40 to 50 minutes or until a toothpick inserted into the center comes out clean. Cool in pan for 10 minutes before removing to cool completely on a wire rack.

Zucchini Bread

1 cup shredded zucchini
1 cup sugar
½ teaspoon lemon juice
1 egg
½ cup vegetable oil
1½ cups all-purpose flour
1 teaspoon cinnamon
½ teaspoon salt
¼ teaspoon nutmeg
½ teaspoon baking soda
¼ teaspoon baking powder
½ cup chopped walnuts, optional
½ cup raisins, optional

This sweet and healthy Zucchini Bread was created out of a surplus of zucchini from my dad's garden and a craving for something tasty. It is simple to make and fills the house with delicious scents of home baking.

Heat oven to 325°. Mix zucchini, sugar, lemon juice and egg. Add oil and mix well. In a separate bowl, mix dry ingredients and add to zucchini mixture. Pour batter into greased loaf pan and bake 65 minutes.

Candace Nelson, Morgantown,
www.candacerosenelson.com

Blueberry Corn Muffins with Lemon Sauce

LEMON SAUCE:

2 teaspoons lemon zest
1½ cups sugar
5 large egg yolks
½ cup fresh lemon juice
⅛ teaspoon salt
½ cup melted butter

BLUEBERRY CORN MUFFINS:

1 cup plain cornmeal
1 cup all-purpose flour
½ cup sugar
2½ teaspoons baking powder
¼ teaspoon salt
1 cup buttermilk
6 tablespoons melted butter
1 large egg, beaten
1½ cups blueberries
½ teaspoon lemon zest

For the sauce, combine zest and sugar in food processor and process until zest is as fine as sugar. Add egg yolks, lemon juice and salt; process 10 seconds. With machine running, add melted butter. Cook in a double boiler over low heat until thick. Refrigerate before serving.

To make the muffins, preheat oven to 400°. Sift cornmeal, flour, sugar, baking powder and salt. Add buttermilk, butter and egg; mix. Carefully fold in blueberries and lemon zest. Divided batter evenly between 12 muffin cups, using paper liners if desired. Bake 20 to 25 minutes or until center pops back when pressed. Serve topped with Lemon Sauce.

Berkeley Microwave Apple Butter

12 to 15 apples, sliced and cored
1 cup apple cider
½ cup sugar per quart of purée
2 to 4 tablespoons cinnamon
1 to 2 teaspoons nutmeg
1 tablespoon molasses

Create apple purée by simmering apples with cider 4 to 6 hours in a pot on the stove. Leave skins on for color but sieve out when finished cooking down the purée. Or you can start with 2½ quarts prepared unsweetened applesauce.

Stir in remaining ingredients. Put into a microwave-safe dish and cover with plastic wrap. Cook 3 to 5 minutes at a time separated by 5 to 7 minute gaps. Stir every time you restart the microwave. Do this for about an hour. Makes 2 to 3 quarts.

Apple Butter Festival, Berkeley Springs

Slow Cooker Apple Butter

Making apple butter in a copper kettle over an open fire remains a weekend community event in this area of Appalachia during the cool, crisp days of fall. Volunteers provide the labor throughout the day to stir the kettle with long, wooden paddles. The method for stirring is to "go twice around the outside and through the middle once" with the paddle. Sometimes copper pennies are added to keep the batch from sticking to the bottom of the kettle. Slow cooker apple butter is surprisingly easy to make. This method requires little stirring, but is sure to stir up thoughts of West Virginia harvest seasons of years gone by.

1½ pounds cooking apples
1 (50-ounce) jar unsweetened
  applesauce
2 cups sugar

¾ cup apple juice
1 teaspoon cinnamon
½ teaspoon cloves
½ teaspoon allspice

Peel and cut apples into small chips. Place all ingredients in a slow cooker and stir. Cover and cook on low overnight, 8 to 10 hours. Remove cover, stir and taste. Add more spices or sugar if desired. Continue cooking for a few more hours, uncovered, until some of the liquid evaporates and butter has cooked down a bit. Pour into jars and refrigerate or can it properly. Serve over hot biscuits, toast, scones, or just eat it out of the jar if no one is looking!

Susan Maslowski, Mud River Pottery, Milton

Berkeley Springs Oven-Baked Apple Butter

15 medium-size apples, 4 to 5 pounds
1½ quarts sweet cider
3 cups sugar, divided
1 teaspoon each cinnamon, allspice and
    cloves
¼ teaspoon nutmeg

Select firm, tart cooking apples. Wash and slice into a large saucepan; do not remove core, seed or peel. Add cider and boil 15 minutes or until apples are soft. Press through sieve. You should have about 3 quarts pulp. Stir in half the sugar and put purée in 2 roasters that will fit in oven. Bake at 325°, stirring every half hour with a wooden spoon. After 1 hour, add remaining sugar and spices. Cook until apple butter is thick and deep brownish red, 3 to 4 hours. Makes 3 to 5 pints.

Apple Butter Festival, Berkeley Springs

Berkeley Springs is home to the Apple Butter Festival , a local and regional must-do event. If you don't have time to make apple butter the old-fashioned way, with family and friends peeling a large number of apples for days, then try this recipe from the Berkeley Springs Chamber of Commerce and the Apple Butter Festival.

Apple Butter Festival
Berkeley Springs
Columbus Day weekend in October

This traditional harvest festival kicks off with a nostalgic hometown parade Saturday morning followed by two-days-worth of family-friendly games and contests, music, country food, fine arts and local crafts. Undisputed star of the Apple Butter Festival is the spicy apple butter stirred in giant copper kettles in the middle of the square. Free admission.

304-258-3738
www.berkeleysprings.com/newtbs/
apple-butter-festival

Stovetop Apple Butter

15 medium-size apples,
    about 4 to 5 pounds
1½ quarts sweet cider
1½ pounds (3 cups) sugar*
1 teaspoon each cinnamon,
    allspice and cloves
¼ teaspoon nutmeg

Berkeley Spring's annual Apple Butter Festival has become well known for its amazing array of tasty apple butters as well as crafts, music, and George Washington. Yep, George Washington, an actor dressed as George Washington serves as Grand Marshall. The Berkeley Chamber maintains a selection of apple butter recipes, including this one.

Select firm, tart cooking apples. Wash and slice into a large pot; do not remove core, seed or peel. Add cider and boil 15 minutes or until apples are soft. Press through sieve. You should have about 3 quarts pulp. Gently boil the pulp 1 hour or until it begins to thicken, stirring occasionally. To save time, you can use 3 quarts commercial applesauce instead of making your own apple purée. Stir in sugar and spices and continue cooking slowly 3 hours or until thickened, stirring frequently. Pour into hot sterilized jars, leaving ¼-inch headspace. Seal. No need to water bath since lids will seal themselves. Makes 3 to 5 pints.

***Note:** To make sugarless apple butter, omit the sugar and choose sweet, not tart, apples.

Jeanne Mozier,
Apple Butter Festival, Berkeley Springs

Sassafras Syrup

2 cups cut sassafras tree root
2½ cups water
2½ cups sugar
1 teaspoon lemon juice

In a small pan, cover roots with water; simmer until you have a deep red tea. Strain to get out bits of bark and root. You should have 2½ cups tea (if not add water to reach that amount). Add sugar. Stir well and bring to a boil. Remove from heat and set aside to cool. Add lemon juice, ¼ teaspoon at a time, until it is as tart as you like. If you like a thicker syrup, simmer longer. Good on pancakes or ice cream.

M. Dawson, Buckeye,
Wild Edibles Festival

Cousin Ann's Apple Cider Syrup

1 cup sugar
3 tablespoons buttermilk
   baking mix
1 teaspoon ground cinnamon
2 cups apple cider
2 tablespoons lemon juice
¼ cup butter or margarine

Mix sugar, baking mix and cinnamon in a 2-quart saucepan. Stir in cider and lemon juice. Cook, constantly stirring, until mixture thickens and comes to a boil. Boil and stir 1 minute. Remove from heat. Stir in butter.

Steve Cotton, Voice of the Thundering Herd,
Marshall University, Huntington

Easy Oatmeal Maple Pancakes

¼ cup maple syrup
1 cup complete pancake mix
½ cup quick cooking oatmeal
Milk as called for in pancake mix directions
1 egg
1½ tablespoons melted butter

This easy recipe is very hearty on a cold morning. The trick is to allow the recipe to rest a few minutes before cooking.

Combine ingredients in a bowl and mix well. Add additional milk if needed to thin or pancake mix to thicken. Cook as you normally would regular pancakes.

Dr. Theresa Regan, West Virginia

West Virginia Maple Syrup Festival
Pickens
Third Weekend in March

The West Virginia Maple Syrup Festival is held the third weekend of March each year in Pickens (Randolph County) offering a weekend of country fun including a famous pancake/buckwheat cake feed with pure maple syrup. A country ham and bean dinner on Saturday evening is followed by an old-fashioned square dance. Saturday and Sunday feature with local musical entertainment throughout the both days with various craftsmen demonstrating their talents and skills. The full schedule can be found beginning in February on pickenswv.squarespace.com. Fun for all ages.

304-924-5363
www.pickenswv.squarespace.com/
maple-syrup-festival/

Walnut Oatmeal Pancakes

1 cup whole-wheat flour
1 cup regular oats, uncooked
½ cup plain cornmeal
1 cup finely-chopped walnuts
½ cup all-purpose flour

1 tablespoon baking powder
4 egg whites
2½ cups milk
¼ cup honey
¼ cup unsweetened applesauce

Mix dry ingredients in a large bowl. Make a well in the center and add remaining ingredients. Mix and let sit at least 10 minutes. Spray skillet or griddle with nonstick spray. Pour ¼-cup batter for each pancake onto the hot surface. Cook until tops are covered with bubbles and edges are cooked. Turn and cook other side. Serve with maple syrup or other favorite pancake toppings. Recipe can be halved.

Kathleen Moran Panek,
Gillum House Bed & Breakfast, Shinnston

Apple Pancakes

1½ cups all-purpose flour
3 teaspoons baking powder
½ teaspoon salt
3 tablespoons sugar
¼ teaspoon nutmeg
⅓ teaspoon baking soda

1 egg
3 tablespoons butter, melted
¼ teaspoon vanilla
1 cup milk
1 cup peeled and grated apples

Combine flour, baking powder, salt, sugar and nutmeg in mixing bowl. In a separate bowl, mix baking soda, egg, butter, vanilla and milk. Combine mixtures stirring only until blended. Fold in grated apple. Bake on hot, lightly greased griddle. When batter is full of holes, turn to brown other side. Turn pancakes only once while cooking. Makes 7 (8-inch) pancakes.

Linda McKay, West Virginia

Bob's Zucchini Pancakes

3 cups grated zucchini
1 teaspoon salt
3 eggs
1 cup grated Parmesan cheese
1½ teaspoons minced fresh mint
3 tablespoons flour
Pepper to taste
Butter or olive oil

This is one of my husband's favorite dishes. The recipe is Turkish in origin, but there are many variations. Served straight from the pan, the pancakes are both savory and sweet. But, I must confess, I've eaten them cold the next day and they are still very good. These pancakes make a great vegetarian meal. I promise, you won't miss the meat.

Mix zucchini with salt and let stand 1 hour. Squeeze moisture from zucchini. Beat eggs. Add zucchini, cheese, mint, flour and pepper. Fry batter in hot butter or olive oil, 1 heaping tablespoon at a time, turning to brown both sides. The pancakes are done when they are lightly browned and crisp on the edges. Makes about 18 pancakes.

Susan Maslowski, Mud River Pottery, Milton

Preston County Raised Buckwheat Cakes

1 envelope dry yeast
1 teaspoon salt
3 cups buckwheat flour
½ teaspoon baking soda
½ teaspoon baking powder
2 teaspoons sugar

In a large bowl, mix yeast and salt into 1 quart (4 cups) lukewarm water and let stand a few minutes. Stir in 2 cups flour then add up to 1 cup more to make a stiff batter. Cover and let stand overnight (or at least 4 or 5 hours). When ready to bake the cakes, dissolve baking soda, baking powder, and sugar in 1 cup hot water. Stir into batter. Add about 1 cup warm water to make a thin batter. Bake on a hot griddle. Save at least 1 cup batter for the next baking. (It will keep in the refrigerator for about a week.) To renew, add 1 pint lukewarm water, ½ teaspoon salt and enough buckwheat flour to make a stiff batter. Recipe makes 8 to 12 cakes.

Preston County Buckwheat Festival

Preston County Buckwheat Festival
Kingwood
Last Thursday in September

The Preston County Buckwheat Festival always starts the last Thursday in September. For more than 70 years, the festival has been entertaining people far and wide. The festival features 3 parades, coronation of Queen Ceres and King Buckwheat, arts and crafts, livestock exhibits, quits, 4H exhibits, Friday night entertainment show, antique car show, a midway with over 20 rides, and festival food including our famous whole hog sausage and buckwheat cake dinners.

304-379-2203 • www.buckwheatfest.com

Breakfast Biscuit Bake Casserole

Now I know this recipe does not have any moonshine in it; I guess it could if you really wanted it in there. You can add other ingredients such as hot sauce, bacon or mushrooms; depends on what you like. This is just a good ole breakfast recipe that's nice on a cold West Virginia morning.

1 (12- to 16-ounce) can biscuits
1 pound breakfast sausage, browned, drained and broken up
Chopped onion and bell pepper, lightly browned in butter
Palm full of chopped cooked ramps, optional
2 cups shredded cheese (I use Cheddar but it's your choice)
4 to 6 eggs, beaten (4 if large, 6 if small or medium)
½ cup milk
¼ teaspoon salt
¼ teaspoon pepper

Treat a 9x13-inch baking dish with nonstick cooking spray. Heat oven to 425°. Flatten uncooked biscuits on a clean plate or flat surface and press onto bottom of baking dish. Press edges together sealing all seams to make a nice solid crust. Spoon in cooked sausage, onions, peppers, ramp and cheese. Mix eggs, milk, salt and pepper in a bowl and carefully pour over sausage and cheese. Bake 15 minutes or until firmly set in center.

A West Virginia moonshiner
who would rather not "be properly identified"

Cheesy Potato Pie

2 cups shredded potatoes
½ (4-ounce) can diced mild chiles
2 cups shredded Cheddar cheese,
    divided
3 eggs
1½ cups milk
1 cup Bisquick
½ teaspoon salt
Pepper to taste
½ tablespoon chopped cilantro

Coat a 9-inch round pie pan with nonstick spray. In a mixing bowl, combine potatoes, chiles and 1½ cups Cheddar cheese. Spread on bottom of baking dish. Combine eggs, milk, Bisquick, salt and pepper and pour over potato layer. Top with remaining Cheddar cheese and cilantro. Refrigerate at least 1 hour or overnight. Bake in preheated 350° oven 45 to 55 minutes or until set. Makes 6 to 8 servings.

Nicholas County Potato Festival
Summersville • September

The Nicholas County Potato Festival celebrates potato farmers in the area with two days of fun for the whole family. You will enjoy amusement rides, a Car and Tractor Show, Farmer's Market, Potato Auction, Pet Pageant, Corn Hole Competition, 5K Race, Spud Hunt and Sack Race, Daily Entertainment, Firemen's Parade, Grand Parade, Potato Idol Competition, Fireworks, Food and Craft Vendors and Mashed Potato, Tater Tot and Hot Wing Eating Contests.

304-872-3722
www.nicholascountypotatofestival.com

Healthy Breakfast Hash

1 tablespoon olive oil
1 cup shredded Yukon Gold potatoes
1 cup baby spinach leaves
2 tomato slices
1 or 2 ounces freshly grated Parmesan cheese
2 lightly beaten large eggs
Pinch of salt and pepper to taste

Heat oil in a medium-size skillet over medium heat. Spread oil around by shaking skillet until it covers bottom. Drop shredded potatoes into center of skillet. Use a spatula to move loose shreds of potato toward middle and then press them flat. Layer with spinach, tomato slices and Parmesan cheese. Pour eggs over hash and cover pan. Once potatoes have started to brown on bottom, about 3 to 4 minutes, carefully flip hash over to finish cooking eggs. Then, flip hash back over onto your plate and season with salt and pepper. Eggs should be browned on bottom. Hash can be folded over itself, similar to an omelet, if desired.

Chad Wood, Bradley

Bacon Ramp Breakfast Quiche

1 (9-inch) pie crust
1 cup cooked crumbled bacon, drippings reserved
1 cup cooked crumbled sausage, drippings reserved
1 or 2 (4-ounce) cans mushroom bits and stems
½ cup chopped ramps, white and green parts
1 (10-ounce) can tomatoes and chiles, drained
6 to 8 eggs, beaten
1¾ cups half-and-half
1½ cups shredded Cheddar cheese
⅛ teaspoon ground nutmeg
Salt and pepper to taste
½ cup chopped parsley

Heat oven to 375°. In a bowl, combine all ingredients, include a tablespoon or 2 of reserved drippings, if desired; mix well. Spoon into pie crust. Bake 35 to 45 minutes or until set and lightly browned. A knife inserted into the center should come out clean. Use foil to protect crust edges if needed towards end of baking time. Allow to cool slightly before slicing.

Dr. Theresa Regan, West Virginia

John's Baked Pineapple Toast

½ cup unsweetened applesauce
1 cup firmly packed dark brown sugar
1 (20-ounce) can crushed pineapple, drained
8 to 10 slices old bread
4 egg whites
2½ cups skim milk
Mint leaves, pineapple chunks, maraschino cherries for garnish, optional

This recipe is low fat, vegetarian, and can be gluten-free if made with gluten-free bread.

Treat a 9x13-inch pan with nonstick spray. Mix applesauce, brown sugar and pineapple; spread over bottom of pan. Trim crusts from bread and cut each slice in half. Place bread on top of pineapple mixture. Mix egg whites and skim milk. Pour over bread and refrigerate overnight. Bake uncovered in preheated 325° oven 30 minutes. Remove from oven and cut between slices into squares. To serve, flip slices over and arrange on a platter. Garnish with mint leaves or pineapple chunks and a maraschino cherry at each end of platter. Serve with warmed maple syrup.

Kathleen Moran Panek,
Gillum House Bed & Breakfast, Shinnston

Green Chile Cheese Grits

4 cups water
1 cup grits or 4 packets instant grits
2 teaspoons salt
½ cup butter
2 (4-ounce) cans chopped green chiles
   or to taste
4 eggs, beaten
1 cup milk
1 teaspoon Worcestershire sauce
1½ cups grated extra sharp Cheddar
   cheese or mixed Mexican-style
   shredded cheese, divided

Linda Hickam, wife of Coalwood, West Virginia author Homer Hickam, offers up this easy-to-make, hearty grits dish. Linda suggests using Mexican-style cheese in place of Cheddar for a different flavor.

Bring water to a boil in a large saucepan. Add grits and salt. Cook until thick, stirring occasionally. Add butter and stir to melt. Reduce heat and add remaining ingredients, except cheese. Mix well. Stir in half the cheese. Pour into a greased 9x13-inch or 10x10-inch casserole dish. Sprinkle reserved cheese evenly over top and bake in preheated 350° oven for 1 hour.

Linda Hickam

SOUPS & SALADS

**Quick West Virginia Chili,
page 65**

Lazy Day West Virginia Beef & Veggie Soup

2½ pounds stew beef, cut into ¾-inch
   pieces
2 (14-ounce) cans ready-to-serve beef
   broth
1 (15-ounce) can chickpeas, drained
1 (14-ounce) can diced tomatoes with
   garlic and onions, undrained
1 cup water
1 teaspoon salt
1 teaspoon dried Italian seasoning,
   crushed
½ teaspoon pepper
2 cups mixed vegetables, fresh, frozen or
   canned
1 cup uncooked ditalini or other small
   pasta
Shredded Italian blend cheese, optional

This easy-to-prepare homemade soup is a complete meal in a bowl. Beef, pasta, vegetables, and assorted seasonings make for a soup that's full of flavor. The West Virginia Cattlemen's Association suggests using fresh West Virginia-raised beef and plenty of fresh vegetables. You can use canned or frozen veggies in a pinch.

Combine beef, broth, chickpeas, tomatoes, water, salt, Italian seasoning and pepper in 4½- to 5½-quart slow cooker; mix well. Cover and cook on high 5 hours or on low about 8 hours. Try not to stir mixture while cooking; leave lid on. An hour before serving, stir in mixed vegetables and pasta. Cover and cook 1 hour or until beef and pasta are tender. Stir well before serving. Top with cheese, if desired.

West Virginia Cattlemen's Association

Savory Chicken or Turkey Vegetable Soup

1 gallon chicken stock
1 pound chicken or turkey, cooked
1 (12-ounce) can tomato paste
1½ cups chopped celery
1⅓ cups chopped onion
½ teaspoon pepper
2 tablespoons dried parsley

1 tablespoon granulated garlic
1 (15-ounce) can whole-kernel corn, drained
1 (15-ounce) can carrots, drained
1 (15-ounce) can green beans, drained
1 (15-ounce) can peas, drained

In a heavy pot, combine stock, chicken or turkey, tomato paste, celery, onion, pepper, parsley and garlic. Bring to a boil. Reduce heat, cover and simmer 20 minutes. Add corn, carrots, green beans and peas. Cover and simmer 15 minutes or until vegetables are tender. Use less stock for a thicker consistency.

West Virginia University Extension Service, Morgantown, www.ext.wvu.edu

West Virginia Penitentiary offers Haunted Tours
Moundville

Chicken and Rice Soup

2 tablespoons olive oil
1 large yellow onion, diced
1 teaspoon crushed garlic
1½ cups sliced carrots
2 stalks celery, diced, plus a few
   leaves
7 or 8 chicken tenderloins, cut into
   ½-inch cubes
1 teaspoon dried thyme or 2
   teaspoons fresh thyme leaves
2 teaspoons curry paste
2 (32-ounce) cans chicken broth
Salt and pepper to taste
1 cup instant rice, white or brown

Heat olive oil in a soup pot. Add onion, garlic, carrots and celery. Sauté until soft, 10 to 15 minutes. Add chicken and stir until golden brown. Add thyme and curry paste; stir in broth. Add salt and pepper. Bring to a boil and simmer gently 30 minutes. Bring back to boil and add rice. Remove from heat, cover and let stand 10 minutes.

Susan's Mulligatawny Soup

1 tablespoon vegetable oil
1 medium onion, minced
1 carrot, minced
½ tablespoon thyme
1½ teaspoons curry powder
2 tablespoons honey
1 pound chicken, cubed
1 large apple (Macintosh is good),
   chopped
1 tablespoon chopped fresh parsley
1 quart chicken stock
2 tablespoons all-purpose flour
1 teaspoon salt
½ teaspoon ground black pepper
1 cup whole milk
2 cups cooked basmati rice

My sister, Susan Cotton Runyon, picked up this recipe in her world travels as a military spouse. The name of this Indian soup, mulligatawny, literally means "pepper water."

In large kettle, heat oil and sauté onion, carrot and thyme until onions are tender but not brown. Stir in curry powder and honey and cook 5 minutes. Add chicken, apple and parsley; stir to coat. Stir flour into a small amount of chicken stock to make a paste. Add to pot with remaining chicken stock, stirring constantly to keep mixture smooth. Add salt and pepper. Simmer 20 minutes. Remove from heat, stir in milk and serve with a spoonful of rice in each bowl. If reheating do not boil or milk with curdle. Makes 8 servings.

Steve Cotton, Voice of the Thundering Herd,
Marshall University, Huntington

Fancy Peanut Soup

1½ cups peanut butter
1 quart milk
½ teaspoon salt
Freshly ground pepper to taste
½ teaspoon vegetable
   seasoning

1 onion, chopped
2 celery ribs, chopped
3 tablespoons butter
3 tablespoons flour
1 quart chicken stock
½ cup chopped peanuts

In a pan over low heat, soften peanut butter to allow for easy mixing with milk. Add milk, salt, pepper and vegetable seasoning. Bring to a boil and then set aside. Sauté onion and celery in butter—do not allow to brown. Stir in flour as if making a gravy. Add chicken stock and stir constantly until mixture comes to a boil. Remove from heat. Combine with peanut butter and milk mixture. Return to stove over very low heat and cook until all ingredients are well blended. Soup may be served either cold or hot. After ladling soup into individual bowls, sprinkle chopped peanuts over top for decoration.

The Honorable & Mrs. John D. Rockefeller IV,
United States Senator, West Virginia

Honey Roasted Butternut Squash Soup

2 pounds butternut squash
2 ounces (¼ cup) olive oil
4 ounces (½ cup) honey
Salt and ground white pepper to taste
1 ounce (2 tablespoons) vegetable oil
2 ounces (¼ cup) chopped shallots
1 tablespoon chopped garlic
6 ounces (¾ cup) diced celery
3 ounces (⅓ cup) diced carrots
12 ounces white wine
3 quarts vegetable stock
8 ounces heavy cream

Peel and seed squash and cut into 1- to 2-inch cubes. Place in a medium bowl, mix with olive oil and honey to lightly coat. Spread squash over a sheet tray and lightly season with salt and white pepper. Roast at 300° about 1 hour or until fork tender. Heat vegetable oil in a medium saucepot over low heat. Add shallots, garlic, celery and carrot. Cook slowly until soft and translucent. Add white wine and simmer 2 minutes. Add cooked squash and vegetable stock. Bring to a boil, and then simmer 1 hour. Purée in blender or food processor until very smooth; strain. Repeat if necessary to achieve desired consistency. Add heavy cream and return to heat; simmer 20 minutes. Adjust seasoning with honey, salt and white pepper to taste. Serve immediately.

Steven Keith, "The Food Guy" columnist for the Charleston Daily Mail

This recipe is from an article I wrote for the Charleston Daily Mail *newspaper when our spring weather was interrupted by a sudden cold spell. I'm a big believer of using leftovers and especially love using leftover turkey, chicken, vegetables, and more (including a homemade stock made from them) in homemade soups and other recipes.*

Mediterranean Potato Bean Soup

1½ teaspoons olive oil
1 clove garlic, minced
½ cup chopped onion
4 cups low-sodium chicken or
    vegetable broth
4 cups water
3 medium red potatoes, unpeeled
    and cubed
3 carrots, sliced
¼ teaspoon ground pepper
2 teaspoons Italian seasoning
1 (15-ounce) can red kidney beans, drained and rinsed
1 cup (2 ounces) whole-wheat noodles, uncooked
2 cups fresh spinach or 1 cup frozen spinach
¼ cup grated Parmesan cheese

This recipe started with a base stock made with the remains of a roasted turkey and lots of leftover vegetables. Adjust the recipe to your own tastes using stock or perhaps bouillon cubes, and feel free to play around by adding some of your favorite ingredients.

Heat oil in a 2-quart pot. Sauté garlic and onion 3 to 4 minutes. Add chicken broth, water, potatoes, carrots and seasonings; cover and bring to a boil. Reduce heat and simmer 15 minutes. Add kidney beans and noodles. Bring to boil again, cook until noodles are soft. Remove from heat. Just before serving, add spinach to pot and stir gently. Ladle into bowls and serve with Parmesan cheese.

Steven Keith, "The Food Guy"
columnist for the Charleston Daily Mail

Burgoo Cook-off

Webster Springs
Columbus Day Weekend

Burgoo Cook-Off in Webster Springs is a fall festival that is fun for the whole family. The star of the show is the Burgoo contest which has an entry fee and pays cash prizes for First, Second, Third, and People's Choice awards. There is no admission to fee to enjoy the fun — live bluegrass music, apple butter making, an apple pie contest, hay rides, cake walks, a scarecrow contest, pumpkin painting, and much more. Bring the family and join the fun.

304-847-7291 • www.visitwebsterwv.com

Beefy Bean Stew

1½ pounds bottom round steak,
    fat trimmed
2 tablespoons flour
1 tablespoon prepared mustard
2 teaspoons chili powder
1 (8-ounce) can tomato sauce
1 teaspoon sugar
½ teaspoon salt
¾ cup water
1 large onion, cut into 6 pieces
1 (15-ounce) can kidney beans

Cut meat into small cubes. In a saucepan mix flour, mustard, chili powder, tomato sauce, sugar and salt; blend well. Stir in meat and water. Bring to a boil over medium-high heat, stirring frequently. Lower heat, cover and simmer 1½ hours, stirring occasionally. Add onion and beans and cook, covered, 30 minutes or until meat is tender.

West Virginia University
Extension Service,
Morgantown, www.ext.wvu.edu

White Chicken Chili

4 boneless, skinless chicken breasts
4 teaspoons vegetable or olive oil, divided
1 onion, chopped
1 teaspoon minced garlic
2 teaspoons ground cumin
2 teaspoons oregano
½ to 1 teaspoon ground cayenne pepper
1 (7-ounce) can diced green Anaheim chiles
2 (15-ounce) cans Great Northern beans or other white beans,
   with juice
4 cups chicken stock or canned chicken broth
1 teaspoon chicken flavor base
1 small bunch cilantro, chopped, about ½ cup (optional)

Trim fat and tendons from chicken breasts. Heat 2 teaspoons oil in a heavy nonstick pan, add chicken and sauté until chicken is cooked through and barely starting to brown. Remove from pan and let cool. While chicken is cooling, heat remaining oil in a heavy soup pot and sauté onion until softened and just starting to brown, about 5 minutes. Add garlic and sauté another minute. Add cumin, oregano and cayenne pepper and sauté a couple minutes longer. Add Anaheim chiles, white beans, chicken stock and chicken flavor base. Turn heat to low and simmer 30 minutes. While chili simmers, use your fingers, fork or mixer to shred chicken into bite-size pieces. (Don't cut with a knife because cut chicken pieces will shred apart into strings in chili when they cook.) After chili has simmered 30 minutes, add chicken and simmer 10 to 15 minutes. If using cilantro, add it to chili at end of cooking time and simmer another 5 minutes. Serve hot.

ChiliFest

Huntington • September

ChiliFest is the West Virginia State Chili Championship sanctioned by the International Chili Society. Cooks from a five-state area come to compete for the state title and go on to compete in the World's Chili Championship. Great chili, spirited competition, live music, games and a Kids Corner event all make ChiliFest a great community event and a fundraiser for the local Ronald McDonald House. To date, ChiliFest has raised over $550,000 for The House.

304-634-4857 • www.chilifestwv.com

Hearty Beef Chili

1½ pounds beef stew meat, cut into 1-inch cubes
2 cups tomato juice
1 large yellow onion, chopped (about 2 cups)
2 (15-ounce) cans black beans, drained
1 (14.5-ounce) can no-salt-added diced tomatoes, undrained
1 large green bell pepper, chopped (about 1½ cups)
1 (10-ounce) can diced tomatoes with green chile peppers, undrained
1 teaspoon ground chipotle chile pepper
1 teaspoon ground cumin
1 teaspoon dried oregano
1 teaspoon salt
3 cloves garlic, minced

Combine all ingredients in a 4½- to 6-quart slow cooker in order given. Cover and cook on low 9 to 10 hours or on high 4½ to 5 hours. Serve hot.

Firefighter Chili

Russ Dean is a member of the West Virginia Beekeepers Association and was a volunteer firefighter for years. He developed this recipe more than twenty years ago. His wife, Angela, says it was great firehouse chili then and it still is!

1 pound bacon
1 medium onion, chopped
1 pound ground beef
2 (15-ounce) cans red kidney beans
2 (14-ounce) cans whole tomatoes
1 tablespoon chili powder
Salt and pepper

Cook bacon, keeping the grease. Crumble bacon in a large pot and set aside. Cook onion in grease until soft; add to pot with bacon. Brown ground beef. Drain and discard grease; add browned beef to pot. Add remaining ingredients without draining the cans. Bring to boil over medium heat. Reduce heat and simmer 4 hours, keeping pot covered and adding additional water if needed.

Russ Dean, Advent

Main Street Martinsburg Chili Cook-Off
Martinsburg • October

Enjoy Music from Clement & Williams and The Eric Chef Group , beer and Chili in downtown Martinsburg. Saturday, October 4th from 2:00 pm to 5:00 pm. to taste chili $5.00 per person, 7 years old and below FREE.

304.262.4200
www.mainstreetmartinsburg.com

Quick West Virginia Chili

3 pounds ground beef (I use 73% lean)
2 tablespoons vegetable oil
2 quarts tomatoes
3 (6-ounce) cans tomato paste
3 (1.25-ounce) packets mild chili seasoning
Dash onion powder
Assorted mixed peppers, deseeded and chopped (sweet bell to as hot as you like)
2 (15-ounce) cans dark red kidney beans, well drained
½ cup fresh or frozen corn off the cob, optional

Brown meat in oil; drain well. Add tomatoes, paste and enough water for a thick consistency but not so thick the chili will catch on the bottom of the pan. Add spices and seasonings; mix well. Add peppers, beans and corn; mix well. Add water, if needed, cover and simmer over medium to medium-low heat at least 30 minutes or until well cooked and flavors are well blended.

Angela J. M. Dean, Advent

Leftover Ham Salad

2 cups finely diced ham
3 hard-boiled eggs, peeled and
    chopped
¼ cup sweet pickle relish
¼ cup mayonnaise
2 tablespoons minced onion
2 tablespoons minced celery

2 tablespoons minced red bell
    pepper
1 tablespoon chopped fresh parsley
2 teaspoons Dijon mustard
1 tablespoon lemon juice
Salt and black pepper to taste
Large pinch cayenne, optional

Combine all ingredients in a large bowl, cover and chill at least an hour before serving.

Linda McKay, West Virginia

Blackwater Falls

First Lady's Cornbread Salad

2 (1-pound) packages Hudson Cream cornbread mix, prepared
    according to directions
1½ cups sour cream
1½ cups Hellmann's mayonnaise
1 (1-ounce) package original Hidden Valley Ranch dressing mix
1 pound bacon, fried and crumbled
3 chopped tomatoes or 3 (14-ounce) cans petite diced tomatoes,
    well drained
1 cup chopped green bell pepper
2 (11-ounce) cans whole-kernel corn
1 cup chopped green onions
2 cups shredded Cheddar cheese

Crumble cornbread into bite-size pieces. Whisk sour cream, mayonnaise
and ranch dressing. Place half the cornbread in a pan. Layer half the sour
cream mixture on top followed by half each of the remaining ingredients.
Top with half of the remaining cornbread, the remaining sour cream mixture
and then all remaining ingredients finishing with remaining cornbread on
top. Refrigerate at least 2 hours before serving.

Governor Earl Ray Tomblin and First Lady Joanne Jaeger Tomblin

Hatfield and McCoy Moonshine Cornbread Salad

2 (15-ounce) cans whole-kernel
   corn, drained
1 (15-ounce) can black-eyed peas,
   rinsed and drained
1 (15-ounce) can black beans,
   rinsed and drained
1 or 2 tomatoes, diced
1 chopped onion, a sweet one if
   you have it
½ (16-ounce) bottle zesty Italian
   dressing
½ cup bacon bits
1 or 2 tablespoons peach moonshine, optional
2 (8.5-ounce) boxes Jiffy cornbread mix plus ingredients for making

Now I'm not saying this recipe ever came from a real Hatfield or a real McCoy. It's just the name we've always called it, although to be honest, I have no idea why. I do know it's a great salad to serve at a summer picnic or cookout with barbecue, chicken, and such. We've made this many times without the shine and just always told people it was in there. They think it's neat.

Combine everything except cornbread mix in a bowl and refrigerate. (Ya'll don't have to use the shine if you don't feel the need or if the kids are coming over. You can save that for sipping later.) Make cornbread using directions on label to prepare as muffins. Cool and crumble cornbread. Just before serving, combine cornbread with refrigerated mixture. Don't want combine too soon or cornbread will get soggy. Serve immediately.

A West Virginia moonshiner
who would rather not "be properly identified"

Easy Pea Salad

1 (15-ounce) can green peas
7 teaspoons sugar
3 hard-cooked eggs, peeled
   and chopped

Salt and pepper to taste
1 small onion, chopped
3 tablespoons salad dressing
5 sweet pickles, chopped

Combine all ingredients; toss lightly. Chill until ready to serve.

Shirley Hyatt,
St. Albans Historical Society, St. Albans

Classic Creamy Coleslaw

8 cups shredded cabbage
1 large carrot, shredded
⅔ cup mayonnaise
¼ cup white vinegar

¼ cup sugar
1 teaspoon salt
½ teaspoon celery seed
¼ teaspoon pepper

Place cabbage and carrot in large bowl. In a small bowl, combine mayonnaise, vinegar, sugar, salt, celery seed and pepper. Pour over cabbage and toss to coat. Cover and refrigerate.

Reba Bolt, Coalwood Community United Methodist Church,
Cooking the Coalwood Way

Honey Coleslaw

1 head cabbage, shredded
1 onion, finely chopped
1 green bell pepper, chopped
½ cup honey

¾ cup olive oil
1 cup white vinegar
1 teaspoon salt
½ cup sugar

In a large bowl, combine cabbage, onion and bell pepper. In a saucepan, combine honey, olive oil, vinegar, salt and sugar. Bring to a boil and stir to dissolve sugar. Remove from heat and allow to cool before pouring over vegetables. Toss to combine and refrigerate until serving. Makes 4 to 6 servings.

Easy Cabbage and Carrot Salad

½ head cabbage, shaved not chopped
1 large peeled carrot, julienne cut
4 tablespoons sugar
3 tablespoons apple cider vinegar
⅓ cup mayonnaise
Salt and pepper to taste

My mom never used the word slaw for this recipe, she always called it cabbage salad. She used the word slaw for finely chopped versions. This is great on bratwurst or smoked sausage.

Combine everything in a bowl and chill 30 minutes before serving. Adjust mayonnaise, vinegar and sugar as needed.

Belinda Morgan, WVU

Old-Time Broccoli Salad

6 cups fresh broccoli florets
½ cup raisins
½ cup sunflower seeds
½ cup cooked, crumbled bacon
¼ cup chopped red onion
⅓ to ½ cup shredded cheese

DRESSING:

1 cup mayonnaise
2½ tablespoons vinegar
¼ to ½ cup sugar to taste

This salad, from my mom's recipe, is one of my favorite game day side dishes when West Virginia plays or for family events from West Virginia to Alabama and Florida. You can make a diet version by substituting peas for the raisins , leaving out the bacon, and using fat-free mayonnaise and a sugar substitute.

Combine broccoli florets, raisins, sunflower seeds, bacon and onion in a large serving bowl; toss to combine. In a separate bowl, whisk together mayonnaise, vinegar and sugar. Add dressing to the salad and toss to mix well; chill thoroughly before serving topped with cheese. Serves 4 to 6.

Barney Gullatt, West Virginia Mountaineers

Garden Fresh Cucumber Salad

2 large cucumbers, peeled and cubed
2 or 3 tomatoes, diced or equal portion halved grape tomatoes
2 stalks celery, chopped
1 (4-ounce) can sliced or chopped black olives, drained
Salt and pepper

DRESSING:
1 (8-ounce) container plain yogurt
⅓ cup sour cream
1 small cucumber, peeled and chopped
1½ tablespoons olive oil
½ tablespoon lemon juice
Minced garlic to taste
Dill powder to taste
Salt and pepper

In a large bowl, mix cucumbers, tomatoes, celery and olives together with a few dashes salt and pepper. In a food processor or blender, combine sauce ingredients and pulse to liquefy. Add additional sour cream or a dash of milk if too thick. Combine sauce with cucumber mixture and gently mix to evenly coat. Cover and chill about 30 minutes. Just before serving toss to recoat and sprinkle with fresh chopped parsley if desired.

Julie DeMary, Monongah

Wilted Lettuce Salad

1 cup red wine vinegar
1 cup sugar
1 bunch leaf lettuce, washed and broken up

Mix vinegar and sugar in a small saucepan. Heat until boiling and sugar is dissolved. Pour over lettuce, toss and serve immediately.

Garden Fresh Salad

2 cups halved cherry tomatoes
4 small cucumbers, cut into
   bite-size pieces
1 small red onion, roughly diced
1 or 2 teaspoons chopped fresh
   basil
1 tablespoon olive oil
2 teaspoons rice wine vinegar
   or vinegar of your choice
Salt and pepper to taste

Summer salads are made from whatever is fresh in your garden, and that doesn't always include lettuce. I try to use the freshest ingredients possible straight from the garden, including peppers, squash, etc. If you don't have a garden, then a farmers market comes in handy.

Mix all together and serve. You may use your favorite dressing instead of the oil and vinegar if you desire.

Pam Branham Miller, Charleston

Easy Blue Cheese Dressing

1 pint sour cream
2 tablespoons vinegar
½ teaspoon each garlic salt, celery salt, pepper and paprika
1 teaspoon salt
¼ cup mayonnaise
½ pound blue cheese, crumbled

Mix all ingredients except cheese, and then carefully fold in cheese. Thin as needed by adding milk.

Shirley Hyatt, St. Albans Historical Society, St. Albans

Molded Waldorf Salad

1 (3-ounce) package lime Jell-O
1 cup boiling water
½ cup cold water
1½ cups unpeeled, diced apples
¼ cup diced celery

¼ cup chopped pecans
1 cup miniature marshmallows
¼ cup mayonnaise
¾ cup whipping cream, whipped

Dissolve Jell-O in boiling water. Add cold water and chill until slightly thickened. Combine apples, celery, pecans, marshmallows and mayonnaise. When gelatin mixture is egg-white consistency, fold in apple mixture. Fold in whipped cream. Turn into a 4-cup mold and chill until firm. Unmold on serving dish and garnish with apple slices, frosted grapes and nuts. Yield 8 servings. Double recipe for a 2-quart mold.

Carol Graley & Ednah Wilson,
St. Albans Historical Society, St. Albans

Morgan's Kitchen Fall Festival

St. Albans
Second Saturday in October

The Annual Morgan's Kitchen Fall Festival, sponsored by the St. Albans Historical Society, is held the second Saturday in October each year at historic Morgan's Kitchen, located along MacCorkle Avenue in St. Albans. Activities include apple butter making, cabin tours, pioneer re-enactors, hit/miss engines, arts and crafts, old time music and antique wood-crafters. Baked goods and hot dogs are available. Apple butter is available for purchase. There is no charge for this event and plenty of parking is available.

304-727-5972
www.stalbanshistory.com/morgans-kitchen

Orange Sherbet Salad

2 (3-ounce) packages orange Jell-O
2 cups boiling water
1 pint orange sherbet
1 (15-ounce) can crushed pineapple, drained
1 (11-ounce) can Mandarin orange slices, drained
2 large bananas

Dissolve Jell-O in hot water. Add sherbet and stir until melted. Add pineapple and orange slices; pour into dish, Slice bananas and place on top then push under surface. Refrigerate until set. Serve as salad or dessert.

Mrs. George L. Dolin,
St. Albans Historical Society,
St. Albans

Eight-Cup Salad

1 cup cottage cheese
1 cup sour cream
1 cup crushed pineapple, drained
1 cup fruit cocktail, drained
1 cup shredded coconut
1 cup miniature marshmallows
1 cup chopped English walnuts
1 cup sliced bananas

Mix together the cottage cheese and sour cream. Add crushed pineapple, fruit cocktail, coconut, marshmallows, walnuts and bananas and mix together. Place in refrigerator to chill.

Note: I guess you would call our version Nine-Cup Salad because we definitely recommend doubling the marshmallows.

Gwen Thomas & the Naylor Family,
St. Albans Historical Society, St. Albans

VEGETABLES & OTHER SIDE DISHES

Cornmeal-Fried Green
Tomatoes, page 87

Kopperston Leather Britches

A mess of leather britches
Bacon grease to taste
Salt and pepper to taste

Place beans in a pan and cover with water. Boil 45 minutes to an hour, until tender. Watch water level while cooking, but near end allow water to cook down (watching to make sure nothing burns). Add seasonings near end of cooking cycle, but continue to cook a little longer so all flavors can meld.

In Kopperston, like many other remote coal mining camps and rural communities, there was a tradition of putting up what you grew each summer. My mother-in-law, Glenna Branham, introduced me to the best green beans I'd ever had before or since. Glenna would string green beans with needle and thread and hang them to dry in a lighted but dry space. For her, it was the upstairs attic window. The name "leather britches" comes from their appearance hanging in the window: like leather britches hanging out to dry on the line.

Cindi Cassis Branham, Charleston

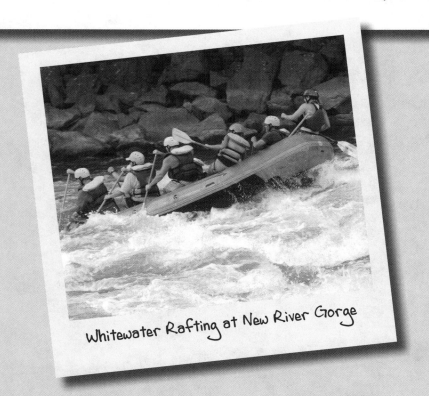

Whitewater Rafting at New River Gorge

Ham Bone "Leather Britches" Shuck Beans

Dried beans
Water
Pork fatback or pork ham bone with
    some meat
Black pepper
Salt

Shuck beans—or leather britches— are dried string beans from the garden. We would string the beans out to dry in the summer so we could have beans all winter long. Mother, from the tiny southern mine town of Cucumber, would cook the beans after soaking them in water overnight, sometimes soaking them twice depending on the bean. About the only seasoning she used was ham bones or black pepper.

Rinse beans and soak overnight in water to cover. Drain and replace water; soak again a couple of hours at the least (longer if you have time). Drain again and replace water. Place pot over high heat and bring to a boil. Reduce heat to medium-low and skim off foam. Cover and simmer 30 to 45 minutes, adding more water if needed. Add fatback and black pepper. Cover and simmer slowly about another hour, stirring as little as possible to avoid breaking up beans. Check for doneness and flavor. Add salt and additional pepper to taste during final 30 minutes of cooking.

Henrietta Anne Foster

West Virginia Cast-Iron Sugar Snap Peas

2 tablespoons olive oil
1 pound sugar snap peas, strings
    removed and rinsed
3 or 4 sliced scallions, green onions,
    or ramps if in season
Salt and pepper
Sugar
Lemon juice
Fresh mint leaves if available

My mom loved her cast-iron skillets. When I married and moved out, I always used more modern nonstick pots and pans. Somehow I could never get the flavor that my mom did when she cooked. It finally dawned on me that certain things, like cornbread, should always be cooked in cast iron!

Heat oil in a large cast-iron skillet over medium-high heat (not too hot as olive oil tends to smoke). Add sugar peas and onions; mix well. Season with salt, pepper and sugar to taste. Cook 4 to 5 minutes then reduce heat. Add lemon juice and mint. Continue to cook, if needed, until beans are done, but still firm and not mushy. Serve hot.

Belinda Morgan, WVU

Ramps & Rail Festival

Elkins
Fourth Saturday in April

Learn about Ramps—the unique, indigenous "wild leek" that grows in the Appalachian mountains—at the annual Ramps & Rail Festival in Elkins. Enjoy local arts, crafts, live music and food vendors who show off scrumptious ramp dishes from 10:00 am to 5:00 pm in the Town Square. Relax on a one-hour ride on the New Tygart Flyer which departs twice on the day of the festival. See website for ticket prices.

877-686-7245
mountainrail.com/special-trains

White Beans and Ramps

2 cups dried white beans, soaked or
    2 (15-ounce) cans white beans
¼ pound ramps, washed and finely
    chopped into thin strips
2 tablespoons olive oil
Salt and pepper
Crushed red pepper

Cook dried beans (or drain canned beans) and set aside. In a skillet, saute ramps in olive oil until wilted. Add beans. (If too dry add additional olive oil.) Stir in salt, pepper and red pepper to taste. Serve hot right from the skillet. Serve with pasta noodles, if desired.

Tommy Atwater and Family,
West Virginia

Greens and Beans

2 tablespoons olive oil
2 cloves garlic, minced
2 bunches kale, chopped
1 cup chicken broth
½ cup turkey sausage or diced
    ham, cooked

1 (15-ounce) can red kidney
    beans or black beans, rinsed
    and drained
Salt and pepper to taste
Parmesan cheese to taste

Heat oil in large sauté pan over medium-low heat. Add garlic and cook 2 minutes. Add kale and sauté 2 to 3 minutes or until kale is cooked down by half. Add chicken broth, a little at a time, to desired consistency. Cover and let ingredients steam on low. Add meat, beans, salt and pepper. Cook until warmed through. Serve warm, topped with Parmesan cheese.

Roasted Summer Squash

6 yellow summer squash or
    zucchini
Olive oil

Lemon or lime juice
Salt and pepper to taste

Position oven rack at top level and preheat oven to 475°. Wash squash and cut off ends. Cut each squash into quarters lengthwise like pickle wedges. Cut each wedge piece in half. If you have a long piece you might want to cut it into thirds. Lightly coat each piece with olive oil and a dash of lemon juice. Sprinkle with salt and pepper or your choice of seasoning. Arrange pieces in a single layer on a nonstick roasting pan. Roast, turning pieces occasionally, 30 minutes or until golden brown. Serve hot.

Andrew Moore, Charleston

Butternut Squash Casserole

1½ to 2 pounds butternut squash
3 eggs
2 tablespoons flour
1 cup rolled oats
2 tablespoons honey
2 tablespoons coconut oil
1 banana
4 tablespoons cinnamon
1 tablespoon nutmeg
1 teaspoon almond extract
Pinch of salt
Pecans for topping

Preheat oven to 450°. Roast squash 45 minutes or until it can be easily pierced with a fork. Reduce oven temperature to 400°. After squash has cooled, about 30 minutes, cut it into chunks and place in a large mixing bowl with everything except pecans. Mash with a potato masher first, then use a hand mixer until everything is thoroughly blended. Pour mixture into an 7x11-inch baking dish and top with pecans. Bake about 30 minutes or until set.

Chad Wood, Bradley

A perfect fall recipe, this dish may not be the prettiest casserole ever made but trust me—it's addictive. You can bake the squash ahead of time if you want.

Kate's Corn Casserole

1 (15-ounce) can whole-kernel
    corn, undrained
1 (15-ounce) can cream-style corn
½ stick (¼ cup) margarine, melted

2 eggs
1 cup sour cream
1 (8.5-ounce) package corn muffin
    mix

Combine ingredients and pour into an 8x10-inch casserole dish. Bake at 350° approximately 45 minutes.

Steve Cotton, Voice of the Thundering Herd,
Marshall University, Huntington

Squaw Corn

2 (15-ounce) cans cream-style
    corn
2 beaten eggs
¾ cup cornmeal
1 teaspoon garlic salt

½ teaspoon baking powder
½ cup cooking oil
1 (4-ounce) can diced green chiles
2 cups shredded sharp Cheddar
    cheese, divided

Mix all ingredients, except cheese, in a bowl. Pour half in a greased casserole dish. Layer with 1 cup cheese and then gently pour remaining corn mixture on top. Smooth corn mixture and top with remaining cheese. Bake uncovered in preheated 350° oven until a knife comes out of the center clean, about 1 hour. Serve warm.

Linda Hickam

Fried Green Tomatoes, Lebanese Style

Olive or vegetable oil
Green tomatoes sliced evenly
Salt

This fried green tomato recipe has its roots in my combined Lebanese-American and West Virginia heritages.

Drizzle a light amount of oil over sliced tomatoes and sprinkle with salt. Cook quickly in a medium-hot skillet being careful not to burn olive oil. Don't move slices around in pan—it will affect browning. Flip with a spatula when first side is browned and tomato appears cooked half way. Don't overcook as you want tomatoes to remain somewhat firm instead of mushy.

Cindi Cassis Branham, Charleston

Cornmeal-Fried Green Tomatoes

1 cup stone-ground cornmeal
1 cup all-purpose flour
1 tablespoon garlic powder
2 teaspoons cayenne pepper
1½ cups buttermilk
Salt and pepper to taste

4 large unripe green tomatoes
½ cup vegetable oil
1 tablespoon unsalted butter
Hot pepper sauce
Lemon wedges

In a large bowl, combine cornmeal, flour, garlic powder and cayenne. Pour buttermilk into a separate bowl and season with salt and pepper. Remove ends of tomatoes and cut into ½-inch-thick slices. Dip tomato slices in buttermilk and then dredge in cornmeal and flour mixture, coating both sides well. Heat oil in a large cast-iron skillet over medium heat. Pan-fry tomatoes, in batches if necessary, until golden brown and crispy, about 3 to 4 minutes on each side. Drain on paper towels. Serve with hot pepper sauce and lemon wedges.

Dr. Theresa Regan, West Virginia

Creamy Mashed and Baked Taters

3½ pounds russet potatoes, peeled and cut into 1-inch cubes
1 (8-ounce) package cream cheese, softened
⅔ cup sour cream
⅓ cup whole milk
¾ cup chopped scallions
½ tablespoon horseradish sauce
½ teaspoon salt
½ teaspoon white pepper
2 tablespoons butter
½ cup shredded mozzarella cheese

Boil potatoes in salted water about 15 minutes or until tender. Drain and mash in a bowl along with cream cheese, sour cream, milk, scallions, horseradish, salt and pepper. Transfer to a greased baking dish and dot with butter. Sprinkle with cheese. Bake in a 350° oven 20 to 25 minutes. Serve hot with additional cheese if you like.

Brad Carter, We Are Marshall

Double-Cooked Canned Candied Yams

¼ cup butter
⅓ cup white corn syrup
2 (15-ounce) cans yams
Pecans

Melt butter in a skillet and stir in syrup. Spoon in yams and stir to evenly coat. Transfer to a glass baking dish and bake at 350° about 20 minutes. Top with crushed pecans and bake another 5 minutes before removing from oven.

Hannah B. Turner, West Virginia

Harvest Festival

Fairmont at Pricketts Fort State Park
Second Weekend in October

Enjoy a fun, fall weekend focusing on 18th century foods. This fun-for-the-whole-family festival includes demonstrations and displays about wild game, food production, harvest preservation, cooking, customs and manners.

304-363-3030 • www.prickettsfort.org

Fried Cabbage and Bacon

6 slices bacon
1 medium onion, thin sliced
1 head cabbage, cored and thick
    sliced
1 tablespoon minced garlic
Salt and pepper to taste
⅛ teaspoon paprika
½ teaspoon onion powder
½ teaspoon garlic powder

My great-grandmother's family was originally from Germany and I'm told this is a variation of German Hot Slaw. You can use link-style sausage, ham, or other meats. A dash of soy sauce gives it an Asian flavor—in this case I use chicken or ham with oil for cooking.

Cook bacon in a large skillet until done but not overly crisp; place on a paper towel to cool. Remove half the bacon fat retaining half in skillet. Add onion to skillet and cook until light brown. Add cabbage, garlic, salt and pepper and cook until cabbage is slightly softened but not too limp. Add paprika, onion power and garlic powder. Crumble bacon and stir into pan. Heat through. (Cook a shorter time for crisper cabbage and longer for softer cabbage.) Serve hot.

Marv and Melanie Henderson, West Virginia

Roasted Cauliflower, Lebanese Style

Cauliflower florets, cut into
   uniform size
Salt to taste
Olive or vegetable oil

Charleston, West Virginia, has a large Lebanese-American population. I'm the second generation born in the United States and I make this recipe often. You can use the same method for potatoes and other vegetables and scale the ingredients to your needs.

Position a rack at very top level and preheat oven to 425°. Place all ingredients in a large bowl and toss until well coated. Spread florets in a single layer on a baking sheet (a nonstick silicon sheet or parchment paper over a perforated tray works best). Place baking sheet on top rack in your oven. Bake 10 to 20 minutes, until golden brown. Remove from oven and enjoy.

Cindi Cassis Branham, Charleston

Pokeweed "Poke Salet" Greens

Leaves from 6 young pokeweeds
1 green pokeweed stem, skinned and
　　chopped into ¼-inch slices
2 cups mustard, collard or similar greens
2 medium onions, chopped
¼ cup bacon fat or lard or 1 piece pork
　　fatback
1 tablespoon maple sugar or molasses
1 teaspoon salt
1 teaspoon pepper
Dash of thyme
2 eggs

My grandmother made Poke Salet and passed her recipe on to me. Our families are from Mississippi, West Virginia, and Eastern Tennessee and every branch of the family had a version of this recipe. I was told you should not eat too much poke as you can get "the belly ache." Always cook poke in multiple changes of water and avoid poke plants that have turned red because they could make you sick.

Rinse poke greens. Cut center ribs and stems out of poke and other greens or pull greens off stems. Chop greens into small pieces and rinse again. Fill a pot half full of water and add poke greens, chopped pokeweed stem and mustard greens. Bring water to a boil and cook 20 minutes. Poke greens should be almost tender. Discard water, rinse and boil again 15 minutes. Drain, rinse, add water plus onions and bacon fat; boil again. As water cooks down, add maple sugar, salt, pepper and thyme. Break eggs into a bowl, beat slightly and put directly into hot, reduced greens stirring quickly to cook eggs and spread them evenly.

Patricia Henderson, Mountaineers Alumni

Taste of Our Towns

Lewisburg
Second Saturday of October

Taste of Our Towns, a benefit for Carnegie Hall, West Virginia, takes place the second Saturday of October each year. Thousands of residents and visitors from across the region converge to gather on the streets of historic downtown Lewisburg to sample delicacies from local restaurants, civic clubs and organizations. Yearly favorites such as The General Lewis Inn's pecan pie and Wolf Creek Gallery's crab cakes disappear quickly. You certainly won't want to miss The Greenbrier who comes out in force with numerous selections from their exclusive restaurants. Cash is not accepted at TOOT. For your convenience, you may order tokens in advance beginning in September. Will-call tokens will be available the day of the event at the Carnegie Hall booth near the green space.

304-645-7917• www.carnegiehallwv.org

Grilled Vegetable Medley

The amounts and variety of vegetables depend on your own tastes and what you can get at your local grocery store. Serve with any favorite meat, fish or as a meal all by itself.

Whole mushrooms
Green, red and yellow bell peppers
White or red sweet onion
Zucchini
Summer squash
Italian dressing

Clean and cut veggies into 1-inch bite-size pieces. Place in a container and coat with Italian dressing. Cover and marinate an hour or so. Grill on a specialty vegetable grilling grate or grilling basket over direct heat with lid closed until tender but still crisp. Depending on number of veggies, this should take about 10 to 15 minutes.

Pryce M. Haynes III, Huntington

Honey Baked Carrots

8 to 10 carrots
3 tablespoons olive oil
⅓ cup honey
Sliced almonds
Salt and ground black pepper to taste
3 to 4 tablespoons parsley flakes

This is my mom's recipe. She preferred fresh carrots when possible, but would use canned when they were on a sale too good to pass up."

Clean, peel and cut carrots into 1- to 2-inch pieces just smaller than a thumb. Place in a baking dish sprayed with nonstick butter-flavored coating. Combine olive oil and honey and stir into baking dish, coating carrots. Sprinkle with almonds, salt and pepper. Bake in preheated 350° oven 45 minutes. After about 30 to 35 minutes I sometimes cover lightly with foil.

Melinda White and Family

West Virginia Honey

Joe's Savory Chestnut Stuffing

1 cup peeled chestnuts
¾ cup diced celery
¾ cup diced onions
½ cup country butter
½ teaspoon sage

1 teaspoon basil leaves
½ teaspoon cinnamon
½ teaspoon sea salt
¾ cup chicken broth
1 loaf white bread, torn into pieces

Sauté chestnuts, celery and onions in butter until glazed. Add sage, basil, cinnamon, sea salt and chicken broth. Simmer 5 minutes. Pour mixture over torn bread and mix well. Pour into a 3-quart casserole dish and bake at 350° until knife inserted in center comes out clean, approximately 35 minutes. (Can also be used to stuff a turkey before baking.)

As remembered by his daughter Martha Nassif Nesser
and his son, N. Joseph Nassif, DDS, Rowlesburg
West Virginia Chestnut Festival

West Virginia Chestnut Festival
Rowlesburg • Sundays in October

Established in 2008 and sponsored by the Rowlesburg Revitalization Committee with the Town of Rowlesburg and Tourism Commission, West Virginia Chestnut Festival celebrates the great American chestnut tree, which originally made-up 40% of hardwood trees in the 16 States of the Appalachian Chain, prior to an Asian blight occurring in the early 20th century. Visitors enjoy sampling and purchasing chestnuts, roasted chestnuts on an open grill, visiting vendors, or attending presentations on restoration of the American chestnut tree. The festival finishes with a gala dinner banquet, featuring chestnut flavored items, and the crowing of chestnut royalty, Mr. and Mrs. Chestnut.

304-329-1240 • www.wvchestnutfestival.com

Coil Spring Zucchini Pasta

1 pound rotini pasta
2 (14-ounce) cans Del Monte zesty-
    style or chili-style tomatoes
3 medium zucchini, cubed
1 pound white cheese, finely
    shredded

As Director of Race Operations for High Performance Heroes, I tend to use racing terms to most aspects of life, including the kitchen. The curled shape of rotini pasta reminds me of parts used to build race cars for our combat-injured veterans.

Boil pasta per directions on package; drain and set aside. In same pot, cook cubed zucchini and tomatoes over low heat, covered, until zucchini is tender. (Sauce should be thin.) To serve, spread a portion of zucchini sauce on bottom of 4 microwave-safe bowls. Layer a portion of pasta over sauce, and coat with additional sauce and cover with cheese. Repeat again to fill up bowls. Microwave 30 seconds to melt cheese. Serve and enjoy.

Ashley Shutka, Director of Race Operations,
High Performance Heroes, Clarksburg,
hpheroes.org

BEEF, PORK & GAME

West Virginia
Whitetail Deer
Stroganoff, page 114

Cast-Iron Skillet Chicken-Fried Steak and Gravy

1½ cups milk plus more for gravy
1 egg
2 cups all-purpose flour
Salt
Pepper
Paprika
Red pepper flakes
4 to 6 hand-size cubed beefsteaks
Oil

I lived in West Virginia for three years and fell in love with the mountains in the summer and fall, not so much during the winter unless I was near a ski slope. When I crave a recipe that reminds me of West Virginia, I either make Chicken-Fried Steak or Pepperoni Rolls. To make this recipe correctly, I suggest using a cast-iron skillet.

Combine milk and egg in a bowl. Combine flour, salt, pepper, paprika and red pepper in a flat plate or foil pan. Dip cubed steaks in liquid and then dredge in flour mixture covering well. Cook in a hot skillet with oil until golden brown. Remove meat from pan, reserving grease and bits and pieces of meat and flour in skillet. Reduce heat to low. For gravy, pour remaining flour mixture into skillet and stir to lightly brown. (If you used all the flour mixture, make more.) The more you brown the flour, the darker your gravy will be. Add milk ¼ to ½ cup at a time, stirring to mix well. Cook over low heat while adding enough milk to make gravy the thickness you like. Add salt and pepper to taste. Plate steaks with potatoes and gravy and a side of hot corn right off the cob.

Scott Anderson, West Virginia

Cattlemen's Sizzling Summer Marinated Grilled Steak

½ cup fresh lime juice
3 tablespoons minced green onions
3 tablespoons water
2 tablespoons vegetable oil
1 tablespoon minced fresh ginger
    or 1½ teaspoons dry
3 large cloves garlic, crushed
½ teaspoon salt
2 pounds high-quality beef top round
    steak, cut 1½-inches thick

For the best flavor, take the time to marinate the meat 6 to 8 hours or overnight. So, plan ahead!

In a small bowl, combine all ingredients, except meat. Combine meat and marinade in a food-safe plastic bag; turn to coat. Close bag securely and refrigerate 6 to 8 hours or overnight, turning occasionally. Remove steak from marinade; discard marinade. Place steak on grill over medium, ash-covered coals. Grill, covered, 25 to 28 minutes to 140° for medium rare; turn occasionally. Transfer to carving board. Let stand 5 minutes. Temperature will continue to rise 5° to reach 145° for medium rare. Carve steak crosswise into thin slices.

West Virginia Cattlemen's Association

My Mama's Meatloaf

½ cup milk
2 slices wheat bread
2 tablespoons olive oil
1 medium onion, sliced
1 package (about 2 cups)
    mushrooms, diced
¼ cup red wine
1½ to 2 pounds ground beef
⅓ to ½ cup Italian seasoned
    breadcrumbs
¾ teaspoon salt
Freshly ground black pepper to
    taste
½ teaspoon ground cayenne red
    pepper
⅓ cup minced fresh flat-leaf parsley
2 eggs, beaten

SAUCE:

½ cup ketchup
⅓ cup brown sugar
4 tablespoons dark molasses or
    maple syrup
¼ cup apple cider vinegar
1 teaspoon ground cayenne red
    pepper or to taste

Preheat oven to 375°. In a large mixing bowl, pour milk over bread slices and set aside to soak. Heat olive oil in a skillet; add onion and saute until translucent. Add mushrooms and cook 3 to 4 minutes. Add red wine and cook until reduced, 5 to 7 minutes. Remove from heat and set aside to cool. To milk-soaked bread, add beef, breadcrumbs, salt, black pepper, red pepper and parsley. Add eggs and cooled veggies. Using hands, mix until well combined. Treat a glass loaf pan with nonstick spray. Form meat into a loaf and place in pan, leaving room on all sides for sauce. Combine all Sauce ingredients. Pour a third on top of meatloaf and spread with a spoon. Bake 45 minutes, and then pour another third of sauce over top. Bake another 20 minutes or until cooked through. Slice and serve with remaining sauce.

Blue Smoke Salsa Cornbread Casserole

1 pound ground beef
½ (9-ounce) jar Blue Smoke Salsa
   (any heat)
1 egg
¼ cup sugar
¼ cup cooking oil
1 cup buttermilk
1 (15-ounce) can cream-style corn
2 cups self-rising cornmeal
1 (10-ounce) package shredded
   Cheddar cheese

I learned how to cook the best way possible, from my mother while trying out recipes in our kitchen. Those are memories that will stay with me forever. When I started Blue Smoke Salsa it was right in my own kitchen perfecting the recipes the way Mom taught me. Blue Smoke Salsa has grown over the last twenty years but the homemade taste is still there.

Preheat oven to 400°. Grease a 9x13-inch pan. Brown ground beef; drain. Combine beef with Blue Smoke Salsa and set aside. In a separate bowl, combine egg, sugar and oil. Add buttermilk, corn and cornmeal. Pour half of cornmeal mixture into baking pan. Top with beef and Blue Smoke Salsa. Cover with Cheddar cheese. Pour remaining cornmeal mixture on top. Bake until golden brown, about 40 minutes.

Robin Hildebrand, President and Founder,
Blue Smoke Salsa, Ansted

Meat Patties

1 pound hamburger
1 onion, chopped
2 to 3 tablespoons lemon juice
Salt and pepper to taste
2 (6.5-ounce) packages pizza
    crust mix, plus ingredients to
    prepare per package directions
12 pats butter

When we were in high school my mother made these from scratch. That means she mixed the dough, covered it for one hour to rise, punched it down, covered it again for another hour. She would make two big bread pans full. I had three brothers and we all loved these hamburgers.

Brown hamburger and onion; drain. While meat mixture is hot, stir lemon juice. Add salt and pepper. Mix pizza crust as directed. Divide into 12 balls. Working with 1 dough ball at a time, place on a flat, floured surface and roll out into a circle. Place 1 or 2 spoons hamburger mixture in center. Fold up sides, closing at top by pinching. Place a small pat of butter on top. Repeat until all dough and meat are used. Place in a single layer on greased baking sheets and bake according to directions for pizza dough. Makes a delicious meal with a tossed salad.

Margaret Bassitt,
St. Albans Historical Society, St. Albans

Braciole

My friend and her late husband would celebrate every wedding anniversary by traveling to an Italian restaurant in southern West Virginia to dine on the house specialty, braciole. Braciole can be cooked with meatballs and Italian sausage in a tomato sauce, which is then served over pasta to accompany the meat bundles. Other cooks add ham or raisins to the filling, altering the recipe to suit their own taste. Several months ago, I decided to make these delicious stuffed meat rolls at home. For ease of preparation, I used slices of beef, sold as Philly beefsteak, which I pounded into thin malleable pieces. The pounding process also helps tenderize the meat. I adapted the recipe for use in a slow cooker.

1 pound Philly steak (or beef round, cut into ¼-inch slices)
Salt and pepper
8 slices prosciutto ham
1 cup shredded fontina cheese
1 tablespoon minced fresh sage
2 tablespoons minced fresh parsley
3 garlic cloves, minced
½ cup breadcrumbs
3 tablespoons pine nuts
Olive oil
1 (10.75-ounce) can beefy mushroom gravy
1 (14-ounce) can diced Italian-style tomatoes

Pound beef slices until thin. Sprinkle with salt and pepper. Place prosciutto on top of each slice. Mix cheese, herbs, garlic, breadcrumbs and pine nuts together. Spread on top of prosciutto. Roll up and secure with toothpicks or string. Heat olive oil in a heavy skillet. Brown braciole on all sides and place in a slow cooker. Top with mushroom gravy and tomatoes. Cook on low 6 to 7 hours. Serve with pasta topped with extra gravy.

Susan Maslowski,
Mud River Pottery, Milton

Border-Lovin' Hot Dog Sauce

2 pounds lean ground beef
1 medium onion, minced
1 cup beef broth
1 cup ketchup
½ cup yellow (or Dijon) mustard
2 tablespoons chili powder
1 tablespoon Worcestershire sauce
1 tablespoon sugar
1 teaspoon crushed red pepper flakes
Salt and pepper

I call it "border-lovin hot dog sauce," because I live and work in the Tri-State area (WV-KY-OH), and this recipe has traveled with me to gatherings and events all across the Tri-State. It is so easy to make.

Begin browning ground beef and onions in a skillet, stir in beef broth and bring to a boil for 5 minutes (breaking up the beef to a fine consistency). Reduce heat, stir in ketchup, mustard, chili powder, Worcestershire sauce, sugar and red pepper flakes. Simmer about an hour, until liquid isn't watery. In the last 15 minutes, salt and pepper to taste. This sauce is great for leftovers, tops about 12 hot dogs, and freezes beautifully.

Kym York-Blake, West Virginia Hot Dog Festival

WV Hot Dog Festival

Huntington
Last Saturday in July (National Hot Dog Month)

Eat your fill of hot dogs while listening to live music and enjoying great entertainment all day at this annual event. You'll love the BUN RUN, BUNS ON BIKES, and HOT DOGS & HOT RODS Car Show. Watch the Hot Dog Eating Contest, Root Beer Chuggin' Contest, and Celebrity Mustard Squirt Contest. Play in the KIDZONE, visit the PETZONE, participate in the all-breed exhibition dog races, annual WV Wiener Dog Races, and $100 "Dachshund Dash" championship race, and so much more. It a full day of family fun benefitting kids in treatment at the Hoops Family Children's Hospital, at Cabell-Huntington Hospital.

304-525-7788 x154 • www.WVHotDogFestival.com

West Virginia Hot Dog Sauce

While there are no set rules on how to prepare hot dogs in West Virginia, we know they are more than just hot dogs on a plain bun. Traditionally, hot dogs come with sauce, mustard, and chopped raw onions or topped with sauce and coleslaw.

1 pound ground beef
1 medium onion, chopped
1 (29-ounce) can tomato sauce
2 tablespoon chili powder or more to taste

Brown ground beef and onion together, chopping meat into small pieces. Drain and return to skillet. Add tomato sauce and chili powder. Simmer over medium-low heat, stirring often, until sauce is desired consistency. Taste and add more chili powder if needed. Stir well. Serve sauce over hot dog in a bun.

Variations: Use ground venison, crumbled veggie burger, ground turkey or chicken, etc., for the meat. Chopped green bell pepper can be added with the onion. Some folks like a splash of Tabasco or hot sauce.

Fran Miller, Parkersburg

Hillbilly Hot Dog Sauce

3 pounds hamburger
2 tablespoons paprika
2½ tablespoons chili powder
1½ tablespoons red crushed pepper
1 tablespoon salt

1 tablespoon celery seed
½ tablespoon garlic powder
1 tablespoon black pepper
1 pint water

Brown all ingredients except water until meat is no longer pink. Add water, cover and bring to a boil. Reduce heat and simmer, uncovered, until most of the water is gone.

Sterling Drive Inn Submarine

Pepperidge Farm club rolls or submarine buns
Cooking oil or margarine
1 pound cooked ground chicken, beef or pork, preferably a mixture of all 3
½ to ¾ cup mayonnaise
Salt and pepper
1 pound bacon, fried crisp
1 (14-ounce) can jellied cranberry sauce
Lettuce and sliced tomatoes

Rub whole rolls with cooking oil or margarine and place in 300° oven to warm. Cut buns open lengthwise. Mix meat with mayonnaise, salt and pepper to taste. Spread scoops of meat mixture onto warm buns. Top with bacon, slices of cranberry sauce, lettuce and tomato. Serve with chips and Coke or Pepsi.

Coalwood Community United Methodist Church,
Cooking the Coalwood Way

Caribbean Burgers with Honey Pineapple Chutney

1 tablespoon vegetable oil
1 ripe fresh pineapple, peeled and chopped
2 large onions, peeled and diced
⅓ cup ThistleDew Farm honey
¼ cup red wine vinegar
1 tablespoon grated orange peel
1 tablespoon grated fresh ginger
¼ teaspoon allspice
½ cup diced red bell pepper
1½ pounds ground beef or turkey
2 teaspoons Jamaican jerk seasoning
½ teaspoon black pepper
6 sandwich rolls or buns, toasted
Butter lettuce leaves

Who says you have to leave West Virginia in order to get a Caribbean-flavored burger? The next time you cook hamburgers try this recipe that combines ThistleDew Farm's honey with spices inspired by the islands.

To prepare the chutney, heat oil over high heat in a heavy, medium-size saucepan. Add pineapple and onions and cook 5 minutes, stirring occasionally. Reduce heat to medium-high and add honey, vinegar, orange peel, ginger and allspice; cook 10 minutes, stirring occasionally. Add bell pepper and cook 10 minutes more; let cool. Makes about 3 cups. In a medium bowl, stir together ground beef, ½ cup Honey Pineapple Chutney, jerk seasoning and pepper. Shape into 6 large flat patties. Grill over medium coals 5 to 8 minutes per side. Serve on toasted buns topped with lettuce leaves and a spoonful of chutney.

Steve & Ellie Conlon, ThistleDew Farm, Proctor

Canadian Bacon Pork Burgers

¾ pound ground pork
½ teaspoon black pepper
1 teaspoon garlic powder
¼ teaspoon salt
4 sandwich buns, toasted
4 slices Canadian-style bacon
4 leaves lettuce
4 slices tomato

Looking for a nice burger with added flavor? Try this pork burger recipe with the added touch of Canadian bacon.

Mix the first 4 ingredients and shape into 4 patties about ½-inch thick. Grill or broil about 4 minutes on each side, until an instant-read thermometer reads 160°. Place patties on bottom half of toasted sandwich buns. Layer on Canadian-style bacon, lettuce and tomato. Top with remaining half of bun.

Jack Yokum and the members of the West Virginia Pork Producers Council

Bear Rocks Preserve

Spanish Pork Casserole

This delicious and easy-to-make casserole is perfect for a family dinner or potluck event.

1 (15-ounce) can garbanzo beans, drained
1 (14-ounce) can Mexican-style stewed
   tomatoes, undrained
1 (6.8-ounce) package Spanish rice mix
1 large onion, halved and thinly sliced
1 red bell pepper, cut into 2-inch by ¼-inch strips
1 cup pimento-stuffed green olives, drained and halved
⅓ cup water
1 clove garlic, minced
⅛ teaspoon pepper
1½ pounds boneless pork loin, cut into 1-inch cubes

Place beans, tomatoes, rice and seasoning packet, onion, bell pepper, olives, water, garlic and pepper in 5-quart slow cooker. Mix until well combined. Place pork over mixture. Cover; cook on low heat 7 to 8 hours or until pork and rice are tender.

Jack Yokum and the members of the
West Virginia Pork Producers Council

Broiled Pork Chops

This is a very hearty pork chop dinner for a cold West Virginia winter or fall night. Serve with rice, pasta, or mixed vegetables.

¾ cup ketchup
¾ cup water
2 tablespoons vinegar
2 tablespoons Worcestershire sauce
2 teaspoons brown sugar
1 teaspoon salt
½ teaspoon paprika
½ teaspoon chili powder
⅛ teaspoon pepper
6 pork chops, bone-in or boneless

In a saucepan, combine all ingredients except pork chops; bring to a boil. Reduce heat; simmer 6 minutes, stirring occasionally. Set aside half the sauce. Place pork chops on broiling pan rack. Broil about 4 inches from heat 4 minutes on each side. Brush with remaining sauce. Continue broiling, turning and basting occasionally, 3 to 4 minutes or until juices run clear. Increase cooking time for really thick pork chops. Serve with reserved sauce.

Hannah B. Turner, West Virginia

Pecan-Stuffed Pork Chops

2 pork chops, at least 1-inch thick
¼ cup breadcrumbs
¼ cup finely chopped onion
¼ cup minced apple
¼ cup chopped pecans
1 small clove garlic, minced
2 tablespoons minced fresh parsley
1 dash black pepper
¼ teaspoon ground mustard
1 tablespoon vegetable oil
¼ cup chicken broth
¼ cup dry white wine

Trim excess fat from pork chops: make a pocket in each by cutting horizontally through to the bone. Combine breadcrumbs, onion, apple, pecans, garlic, parsley, pepper, mustard and oil; mix well. Divide mixture and fill each pocket with as much stuffing as possible. Place pork chops in a greased baking dish. Pour broth and wine over chops. Add leftover stuffing (if there is any). Bake at 350° at least an hour or until tender, basting occasionally. Serve with rice or potatoes.

*Governor Earl Ray Tomblin and
First Lady Joanne Jaeger Tomblin*

Governor Earl Ray Tomblin and First Lady Joanne Jaeger Tomblin spend time in the kitchen preparing Pecan-Stuffed Pork Chops. While time is limited during the work week, they still love creating homemade meals together whenever possible. In addition to home cooking, the First Lady is also known for her work with West Virginia food banks, visits to community kitchens, and aid during emergency relief efforts. She is even coming out with her very own cookbook later this year, and the contributions from its sales will be donated to Mountaineer Food Bank, which serves over six-hundred programs in forty-eight counties in West Virginia. "I truly believe in giving back. Sharing the gift of your time and talents to help others is not only a valuable learning experience, it helps to build a stronger community and state," First Lady Tomblin said.

Venison Jerky

1½ to 2 pounds venison
1 (1-ounce) package instant meat
    marinade
1¾ cups cold water
½ teaspoon liquid smoke
¼ teaspoon garlic powder
¼ teaspoons onion powder
¼ teaspoon black pepper
½ teaspoon Tabasco sauce

While my family does not eat wild game often, one food that I'll never turn down is deer jerky. My grandma makes this from time to time, and all the grandchildren fight over the batch.

Cutting with the grain, slice venison into strips 6 inches long, 1½-inches wide and ½-inch thick. Set aside. Mix together remaining ingredients. Place meat in container and cover with marinade, piercing meat slices deeply with fork. Marinate overnight in a covered container in refrigerator. Remove meat strips, drain slightly and place on rack, making sure strips do not overlap. Place rack over a cookie sheet in a 150° to 175° oven and bake 3 to 3½ hours. Remove from oven, cool and store in a covered container in refrigerator. Since this jerky does not have preservatives like the commercial products, it is necessary to keep it under refrigeration.

Candace Nelson, Morgantown,
www.candacerosenelson.com

Dad's Fried Venison Steak

Our family calendar contains several major holidays: Christmas, Thanksgiving, Easter, the Fourth of July, and the opening day of deer season. A successful deer season means the chest freezer is full and there will be good eating until next fall: venison burger, venison stew, venison jerky—and best of all—Dad's fried venison steak. All of the credit for this dish goes to my dad, Glenn Cotton.

Flour
Crushed saltine crackers
Pepper
Seasoning salt
Trimmed venison, cut thin
Bacon grease or olive oil for frying

Mix dry ingredients and pound into steaks with a meat hammer. (Really mash it to a pulp.) Quick-fry steaks in a hot skillet in bacon grease or olive oil.

Steve Cotton, Voice of the Thundering Herd,
Marshall University, Huntington

Venison and Blue Cheese

¼ to ½ pound blue cheese
5 pounds ground venison
1 or 2 spring or green onions, chopped
2 cups breadcrumbs or cracker crumbs
1 cup sour cream
Salt and pepper to taste

Crumble blue cheese. Mix together cheese, meat, onions, breadcrumbs and sour cream. Salt and pepper to taste. Roll mixture into balls and fry. This is a different meatball for spaghetti, or they can be used as a meat course. Serves 6.

West Virginia Division of Natural Resources,
South Charleston

West Virginia Whitetail Deer Stroganoff

1 pound deer stew meat
1 medium onion, cut into rings
8 ounces portobello mushrooms, sliced
2 (10-ounce) cans cream of mushroom soup
½ cup Worcestershire sauce
1 drop Texas Pete hot sauce
16 ounces sour cream
1 (16-ounce) bag egg noodles

Brown meat in a Dutch oven. Stir in onion rings and mushrooms and cook until caramelized. Add soup, Worcestershire sauce and hot sauce. Boil water for noodles. When water is boiling, add sour cream to deer meat mixture. Simmer gently; do not boil. Cook noodles in boiling water as per packaging directions. Serve stroganoff over hot noodles.

West Virginia Division of Natural Resources, South Charleston

Smothered Rabbit and Onions

1 rabbit, cut into small pieces
Salt to taste
Paprika to taste
Flour
3 tablespoons butter
1 or 2 onions, sliced
1 cup sour cream

Season rabbit with salt and paprika. Coat with flour. Melt butter and sauté rabbit until brown. Cover rabbit thickly with onion slices. Sprinkle onions with salt. Pour in sour cream. Cover skillet and simmer 1 hour or bake at 325° until tender.

West Virginia Division of Natural Resources, South Charleston

Baked Wild Turkey

1 wild turkey
Salt and pepper to taste
Garlic powder or garlic salt to taste
2 to 4 cups water

To prepare turkey, salt and pepper lightly. Sprinkle with garlic powder or garlic salt. Place bird in a baking pan. Add water, cover tightly and bake at 350° until tender, approximately 3 hours. Since wild turkey has a tendency to be a bit dry, slice all meat from bones and pour broth over meat to serve.

West Virginia Division of Natural Resources, South Charleston

West Virginia Turkey Festival
Mathias
Fourth Weekend in October

West Virginia Turkey Festival is held to honor Turkey growers in the state. The festival features a turkey/ham dinner, turkey shoot, car show, craft show, pageant and other events. Everyone is welcome to come see the beautiful little town of Mathias and enjoy everything the festival has to offer.

304-897-7282
www.facebook.com/
wvturkeyfestivalpageant

Barbecued Bear

3 pounds bear steak
2 tablespoons vegetable oil
1 cup ketchup
⅓ cup steak sauce
2 tablespoons tarragon vinegar

1 tablespoon lemon juice
1 onion, diced
½ teaspoon salt
1 tablespoon chili powder

Trim all fat from bear steak and cut meat into 2-inch cubes. Brown meat on all sides in oil in a heavy skillet, then place in a casserole dish. Add remaining ingredients to fry pan and bring to boil, stirring constantly. Pour sauce over meat in casserole dish. Cover and bake at least 2 hours at 325°, stirring occasionally, until meat is tender. Be sure meat is well done before eating.

West Virginia Division of Natural Resources, South Charleston

Williams River
Monongahela National Forest

Bear Roast Marinade

3 cups water
1½ cups vinegar
2 cups red wine
½ cup olive oil
3 bay leaves
½ teaspoon sage
¼ teaspoon allspice
¼ teaspoon nutmeg
½ teaspoon red pepper
1 teaspoon dill seed
1 teaspoon paprika
1 teaspoon garlic salt
1 cup finely chopped onions
1 cup finely chopped celery
½ stick (¼ cup) butter plus extra for
    rubbing on roast
2 tablespoons salt
1 tablespoon pepper
1 (10-pound) bear roast
6 to 8 whole cloves

The black bear is actually deeply tinted with brown. One or two cubs, and on a rare occasion three, are born at a time, each weighing about eight ounces. The adult reaches an average weight of 250 pounds. The black bear became the official state animal on March 23, 1973. The black bear population has steadily grown in West Virginia with bear sightings reported in every county in the state. The West Virginia Division of Natural Resources (DNR) allows for hunting of black bear during certain times of the year with the proper license. Limits and other regulations are subject to change so the DNR suggests checking before hunting.

Combine all ingredients except meat and cloves and simmer 30 minutes. Before marinade cools, add meat and allow to marinate overnight in refrigerator. Next day, remove roast from marinade, rub a little butter over roast and stick in cloves. Place meat and marinade in a roaster and cook 30 minutes per pound in a slow 325° oven. Bear has the consistency of pork and should be served well done. About 3 minutes before roast is done, pour off marinade and thicken to make a gravy. Serve with sweet potatoes and sauerkraut or a good spicy coleslaw. Bear meat is very rich, so this recipe will serve 14.

West Virginia Division of Natural Resources,
South Charleston

Squirrel and Dumplings

SQUIRREL:

1 large squirrel, skinned
Salt and pepper
1½ cups milk
1 stick butter

Place squirrel in a large stockpot with water to cover. Season heavily with salt and pepper. Bring to a boil and cook until fork tender, about 20 to 30 minutes. Reduce heat to simmer. Remove squirrel and set aside to cool. Add milk and butter to broth and continue to simmer while making dumplings.

DUMPLINGS:

4 cups self-rising flour
3 tablespoons butter-flavored Crisco
2 cups buttermilk

Sift flour. Cut in Crisco to resemble coarse meal. Add buttermilk, a little at a time, until dough resembles biscuit dough. Roll dough, working in 3 or 4 batches, to about ⅛-inch thick. (If dough is too sticky add more flour.) Cut into 1-inch squares with a knife. Return broth to a full boil. If pot is less than ½ full, add water or chicken broth. Drop dumplings into boiling broth one at a time. When all dumplings have been added to the pot, reduce heat to simmer. Cover and cook an additional 15 minutes. Pull squirrel meat from bone and add to pot.

Squirrel with White Gravy

4 squirrels
Water
Salt and pepper to taste

Flour
½ stick butter
Hot biscuits

Cut each squirrel into 4 pieces. Place in heavy pot. Add enough water to cover squirrels well. Add salt and pepper. Boil slowly until squirrels are tender. Remove all pieces of squirrel from stock. Roll each piece heavily in flour; gently drop back into boiling stock. Add butter and cook slowly until stock has thickened to gravy. Serve over hot biscuits.

West Virginia Division of Natural Resources, South Charleston

Autumn Harvest Festival & Roadkill Cook-Off

Marlinton
Last Saturday in September

The West Virginia RoadKill Cook-off is one of the region's most fun and exciting annual events covered in years past by the Food Network, the Travel Channel and the Discovery Channel. If you've ever wanted to taste exotic dishes like squirrel gravy over biscuits, teriyaki-marinated bear or deer sausage, this is the place to be. This wild and offbeat festival is guaranteed fun for the entire family, so come see what Andrew Zimmern from Bizarre Foods calls "The Real Deal."

800-336-7009 • pccocwv.com/roadkill

Moonshiner Grilling Sauce

1 (18-ounce) bottle barbecue sauce
1 (10-ounce) jar peach preserves
¼ cup peach-flavored moonshine
¼ teaspoon cayenne pepper

Combine everything in a saucepan and simmer 10 minutes. (Don't boil.) Use immediately or cool and store in the fridge. If you don't have moonshine, try bourbon or whiskey. The flavor's not exactly the same, but it still tastes good.

A West Virginia moonshiner
who would rather not "be properly identified"

Mountaineer White BBQ Sauce

1½ cups mayonnaise
¼ cup white wine vinegar
1 tablespoon coarsely ground pepper
1 tablespoon Creole mustard
1 teaspoon salt
2 minced garlic cloves
2 tablespoons prepared horseradish

Whisk all ingredients until well blended. Store covered in the refrigerator. Great with hot wings, fried chicken, beef, etc.

Larry Meador, Hinton, www.tailgatewvu.com

Hogging Up WV BBQ & Music Festival

Great Cacapon
Fourth Weekend in October

West Virginia State Championship BBQ & Music Festival is a two-day event in the mountains of West Virginia. Held at Cox Camping just 12 miles outside Berkeley Springs, nestled at the foothills of the Cacapon mountains, you will enjoy the beauty of West Virginia and a wonderful weekend in the wilderness along with music, barbecue and more food, vendors, beer and more. As seen on *The Rachael Ray Show*, and in the *New York Times*, Steven Raichlen's barbecue books and *Saveur* magazine.

410-908-9241 • www.HoggingUpWV.com

Larry's BBQ Sauce

My BBQ sauce is a staple ingredient when tailgating at West Virginia Mountaineer football games and for other occasions. I use this sauce with my smoked pork shoulder. The recipe is easy to follow and the sauce turns out tasty every time. Use less red pepper for a mild sauce, more if you want it spicier.

1 gallon tomato sauce
2 (12-ounce) cans tomato paste
4 tablespoons Wright's Liquid Smoke
2½ tablespoons salt
1 tablespoon black pepper
1 tablespoon minced garlic
½ tablespoon onion powder
1½ cups apple cider vinegar
¼ cup honey
¼ cup molasses
2 tablespoons prepared mustard
1 teaspoon red pepper or to taste
1 medium onion, chopped
1 teaspoon paprika
½ teaspoon ground celery seed

Mix all and simmer for a while, at least until you can't stand to smell the wonderful aroma any longer, then ya' gotta eat it.

Larry Meador, Hinton,
www.tailgatewvu.com

Roy's Barbecue

1 Boston butt pork roast, small enough
   to fit in a slow cooker
1 large onion, chopped or diced
1 cup water
Salt, pepper and garlic to taste
1 cup (more or less to taste) barbecue
   sauce, I like Carolina Treat

This recipe is from Rocket Boy Roy Lee Cooke, who was born in Coalwood in the left half of the first double house north of the old school bridge on Christmas Day, 1941.

Cook pork, onion, water, salt, pepper and garlic 6 to 9 hours in a slow cooker set on low. I put mine on at bedtime. Next morning, remove any bone and especially the fat. Add barbecue sauce and cook over low heat a couple hours longer. If you do this upon getting out of bed, it will be ready in time for a great brunch.

Roy Lee Cooke, Coalwood Community United Methodist Church,
Cooking the Coalwood Way

Ribfest BBQ Festival
Charleston • September

The annual Ribfest BBQ Festival features world-class award-winning barbecue rib vendors from around the country serving the best barbecue ribs, chicken and sauces you will ever eat along with a variety of other great foods including Philly cheesesteaks, hamburgers, hot dogs, seafood and a selection of delicious desserts. People come from over 12 states to enjoy the great foods and entertainment including carnival rides, nightly entertainment, attractions, petting zoo, pony rides, eating contest and much more. This family friendly event has lots to do for people of all ages.

304-444-2921 • www.charlestonwvribfest.com

Pomegranate Bourbon Glaze

¼ teaspoon minced garlic
¼ teaspoon minced shallot
½ cup bourbon
½ cup pomegranate juice
1 tablespoon honey
1 tablespoon slurry of
    cornstarch and water
Salt and pepper to taste

Sweat garlic and shallot until translucent in medium saucepan. Add bourbon and reduce by half. Be careful, bourbon can flame. If bourbon flames, set a larger sauté pan on top of saucepan so that flame goes out. Add pomegranate juice and reduce by half. Add honey. Add slurry in small increments to thicken. Add salt and pepper to taste.

Tamarack: The Best of West Virginia, Beckley, www.tamarackwv.com

RC Cola Steak Sauce

1 (12-ounce) can cola, regular
    not diet
1 cup ketchup
⅓ cup steak sauce
Juice and zest of 1 lemon
½ teaspoon ground ginger
Salt and pepper to taste
Dash hot sauce

Mix ingredients in a saucepan and simmer over medium heat but do not bring to a full boil. You want to gently reduce the liquid until the sauce thickens a bit.

Hannah B. Turner, West Virginia

Chipotle Cola Reduction

1 teaspoon minced fresh garlic
1 teaspoon minced fresh shallot
1 teaspoon olive oil 1 (12-ounce) can
   regular cola, not diet
¼ cup apple cider vinegar
½ cup puréed smoked jalapeño
   (chipotle) peppers
¼ cup ketchup
1 teaspoon cornstarch in 1 cup water
Salt and pepper to taste

This simple recipe for a reduced sauce can be used in a multitude of ways and on a variety of foods. It is wonderful on pork, chicken, and even fresh garden vegetables roasted on the grill, oven or skillet.

In medium saucepan, sweat garlic and shallot in olive oil. Be sure not to burn. Cook until translucent. Add cola and vinegar; reduce by half. Add chipotle purée and ketchup. Bring to a simmer. Add cornstarch mixture and cook until thickened. Finish with salt and pepper.

Tamarack: The Best of West Virginia, Beckley,
www.tamarackwv.com

CHICKEN

**Cilantro Lime Marinated
Grilled Chicken Breast,
page 129**

Brick-Pressed Lemon & Thyme Grilled Chicken

4 lemons, juiced and zested
10 sprigs fresh thyme
5 cloves garlic, minced
2 cloves shallots, minced
Sea salt to taste

Black pepper to taste
1 cup blended oil
1 whole chicken, backbone and neck
  removed

Mix lemon zest and juice, thyme, garlic, shallots, salt, pepper and oil. Toss chicken in marinade and refrigerate overnight. Remove chicken from marinade and pat dry with towel. Season both sides with salt and pepper. Heat grill to medium-high. Place chicken on grill and flatten with a foil-wrapped brick or iron skillet. Leaving brick or skillet in place, cook chicken 15 minutes. Turn chicken over, replace brick or skillet and cook another 15 minutes. Remove from grill when chicken has reached an internal temperature of 165°. Allow it to rest 10 minutes before serving.

Tamarack: The Best of West Virginia, Beckley, www.tamarackwv.com

Tamarack: The Best of West Virginia Artisan Retail Center

Mamaw's Roasted Whole Chicken

1 whole roasting chicken
Salt and pepper
1 lemon
Onion slices
Fresh herbs
Garlic powder
Olive oil

This is my family's roasted chicken recipe. My dad says his mom would add fresh herbs depending on what she had at the time. Dad used Italian seasoning but I prefer herbs as well, using rosemary and thyme from my own garden or the market.

Rinse and clean chicken, removing neck, giblets and any excess fat. Place chicken in a roasting pan and season with salt and pepper. Slice lemon in half and juice over chicken. Place lemon and onions in chicken cavity. Place herbs into cavity and sprinkle with garlic powder. Rub outside of chicken with a small amount of olive oil and sprinkle with additional pepper and garlic powder, if desired. Bake in a preheated 425° oven 20 minutes. Reduce temperature to 375° and cook an additional hour. Cover any blackened edges, or whole chicken, lightly with foil if needed during the last 15 minutes. Cook until juices run clear and internal temperature reads 165°.

Melinda White

Mom's Hot Fried Buttermilk Chicken

1 whole chicken, cut up
Salt and pepper
Buttermilk
Hot sauce
All-purpose flour
Oil for frying

This is my mom's fried chicken recipe. According to her, the key to the recipe is soaking the chicken at least 30 minutes in the buttermilk and hot sauce. She made it with hot sauce because my dad loved anything with a little bit of heat.

Season chicken with salt and pepper. In a glass baking dish or zip-close bag, mix buttermilk and hot sauce to taste. (I use 2 to 3 tablespoons for 1 chicken.) Add chicken pieces and turn a couple of times to evenly coat. Refrigerate 30 minutes or longer. When ready to cook, dredge each piece in flour and cook in hot oil in a large cast-iron skillet over medium heat. Cook until meat is no longer pink inside and juices run clear, turning as needed until golden brown all over. Rest on a paper towels, wire rack or paper bag about 5 minutes before serving.

Tommy Atwater & Family, West Virginia

Cilantro Lime Marinated Grilled Chicken Breast

1 cup fresh lime juice
Juice from 1 fresh lemon
¼ cup olive oil
⅛ cup raspberry vinegar
1 cup chopped fresh cilantro

2 garlic cloves, minced
1 jalapeño, minced
5 or 6 (8-ounce) chicken breasts
Salt and pepper to taste

Combine lime juice, lemon juice, olive oil, raspberry vinegar, cilantro, garlic and jalapeño in a mixing bowl. Place chicken in a large zip-close bag and pour marinade over chicken. Squeeze all air from bag before sealing and refrigerate 4 hours. Remove chicken from bag and dry completely with paper towels; season to taste with salt and pepper. Place reserved liquid into a small pot. Bring to a boil and reduce heat. Preheat grill to medium high. Place chicken on grill offset so that it is not directly over flame. Close lid and roast 20 to 25 minutes. Turn frequently and move chicken around so each piece has equal time near heat source. Use boiled reserved liquid as a baste, drizzle sauce or serve on the side.

Tamarack: The Best of West Virginia, Beckley,
www.tamarackwv.com

Baked Pecan Chicken Breast

6 boneless, skinless chicken
    breasts, pounded thin
4 cups ice water and ice
4½ teaspoons salt, divided
2 tablespoons milk
2 tablespoons honey
2 eggs, beaten
½ teaspoon coarsely ground
    fresh black pepper
¾ cup pecan meal

Marinate chicken breasts 30 minutes in ice water mixed with 4 teaspoons salt. In a shallow bowl, beat milk with honey; add eggs. Add remaining salt and black pepper. Put pecan meal in separate bowl. Dip each chicken breast in egg wash and then into pecan meal, patting meal into breast to form a crust. Place breasts in a shallow baking pan that has been sprayed with nonstick cooking spray and bake 35 minutes at 375° or until breasts are done through.

West Virginia Beekeepers Association

South West Virginia Chicken

4 to 6 boneless chicken breasts
4 to 6 slices provolone cheese
1 (16-ounce) jar Blue Smoke Salsa, any heat
1 cup chopped green onions

Grill chicken and top with cheese. After cheese has melted, top with Blue Smoke Salsa and onions. Serve over rice.

Robin Hildebrand, President and Founder,
Blue Smoke Salsa, Ansted

Chicken Crescents

4 boneless, skinless chicken breasts
1 teaspoon sage
Salt and pepper to taste
1 (8-ounce) package cream cheese,
    softened and cut into small pieces
2 (8-ounce) cans crescent rolls
1 stick (½ cup) margarine, melted
1 (6-ounce) package stuffing mix,
    crushed

Bill Lilly says that this recipe, from his family collection, was perfected over the years by Anna Lilly, Josiah Lilly Line, and Jim Bench Line. Their family has huge reunions and one year they set a record in the Guinness Book of World Records with a reunion that topped 5,000 family members. "That's bigger than the West Virginia State Fair back in the 40's!"

In a pot, cover chicken with water, add sage, salt and pepper and simmer until meat is tender. Remove chicken from liquid. Shred meat coarsely. Combine chicken and cream cheese while chicken is still warm. Chill in refrigerator. Remove rolls from cans and separate. Press each crescent roll until it is large enough to hold a portion of chicken mixture. Put an equal scoop of chilled chicken mixture into each crescent and roll up, stretching dough to seal in chicken. Spoon melted margarine over each roll, coating well. Roll each crescent roll in crushed stuffing mix. Place rolls on a greased cookie sheet and bake at 400° about 20 minutes. Serve with gravy over top.

Bill Lilly, Lilly and Line Families,
Jumping Branch

Chicken Cacciatore

1 chicken, cut-up
Salt and black pepper to taste
¼ to ½ cup extra-virgin olive oil
4 large onions, sliced and separated
    into rings
3 large garlic cloves, chopped
3 cups dry vermouth
2 cups chicken stock
1 quart skinned fresh tomatoes
    or 1 (32-ounce) can San Marzano
    tomatoes
2 tablespoons Italian dressing
½ teaspoon crushed red pepper
1 teaspoon kosher salt
1 teaspoon black pepper

Season chicken liberally with salt and pepper. Heat a large braising pan to medium heat and add olive oil. When oil begins to shimmer, add chicken and brown on all sides. Remove chicken and place on a plate lined with paper towels. Working quickly, add onion rings and cook until onion rings are slightly golden. Add garlic and sauté, stirring with a wooden spoon until garlic is translucent. Add dry vermouth and bring to a simmer. Add chicken, chicken stock, tomatoes, Italian dressing, red pepper, and kosher salt and black pepper. Cover with parchment paper and then lid of braising pan. Place in a 325° oven 1 hour and 30 minutes. Serve with buttered pasta or steamed rice.

Tamarack: The Best of West Virginia, Beckley,
www.tamarackwv.com

Spicy Sweet Glazed Chicken with Tangy Relish

¼ cup chopped red bell pepper
1 seedless orange, peeled and chopped
1 small pear, cored and chopped
2 tablespoons chopped fresh cilantro
2 tablespoons orange juice
½ cup honey
1 (11-ounce) can chipotle chiles in adobo sauce
4 boneless chicken breasts
4 cups steamed rice

For the relish, mix first 5 ingredients in a medium bowl and set aside. Put honey in another bowl for the glaze. Finely chop 1 chipotle chile and mix into honey with 2½ tablespoons adobo sauce. (Refrigerate remaining chipotle chiles and sauce for another use.) Set aside 1 tablespoon honey glaze mixture. Brush half of remaining glaze over 1 side of each chicken breast. Place in a broiler pan glaze side up. Broil about 6 inches from heat 6 minutes. Flip chicken and brush with other half of glaze. Cook another 6 or 7 minutes until juices run clear. Drizzle last tablespoon of glaze over chicken. Serve over steamed rice and top with relish.

West Virginia Beekeepers Association

Ramp-Wrapped Chicken Breasts

I'm not really a cook but during ramp season this recipe is a favorite. If it's not wild ramp season you can use long green onions or scallions. I've used chicken thighs, tucking the edges of the ramp under the skin to hold it in place. With drumsticks, you can actually tie the scallion or onion in a loose knot.

4 to 6 bone-in chicken breasts with skin
1 stick butter, melted
Lemon juice
Salt and pepper
4 to 6 ramps, trimmed and rinsed
Italian dressing

Rinse and dry chicken. Combine butter and lemon; brush over chicken. Season to taste with salt and pepper. Wrap a ramp around each piece. Large breasts may require a toothpick to secure the ramp. Grill over medium-high heat turning as needed until chicken juices run clear. About 5 minutes before removing from grill, baste with Italian dressing.

Tommy Atwater & Family, West Virginia

Martinsburg Chocolate Festival and Book Fair
Martinsburg
Last Weekend in April

Indulge the mind and the senses at the Fourth Annual Chocolate Fest/Book Faire held in historic downtown Martinsburg West Virginia on the last weekend of April. Experience a one day Extravaganza held throughout downtown businesses. Explore the unique shops and speak with West Virginia Authors, tours at DeFluri's Fine Chocolates, Chocolate Cupcake Contest, Willy Wonka & The Chocolate Factory showing at the Public Library and much more.

304-262-4200
www.mainstreetmartinsburg.com

Chipotle Chocolate Mole Sauce

I'm a bit torn on whether this very tasty mole sauce tastes better on chicken or beef, so why not try it on both and decide for yourself. I recommend using low-sodium, low-fat chicken broth and unsalted almonds to reduce the sodium content because most store-bought seasoning packets are already loaded with sodium.

⅓ cup sesame seeds
½ teaspoon cumin seeds
2 tablespoons olive oil
3 garlic cloves
3 whole cloves
1 small cinnamon stick
⅓ cup chopped cilantro
5 whole medium tomatoes
1 small onion, coarsely chopped
4 cups low-sodium, low-fat chicken broth
1 (1.25-ounce) package chipotle taco seasoning
½ cup sweet corn kernels
3 ounces unsweetened baker's chocolate, melted
⅓ cup toasted pumpkin seeds
20 whole unsalted almonds
1 pound chicken (and/or beef) strips
Salt and ground black pepper

Toast sesame seeds and cumin seeds in a dry skillet. Add olive oil, garlic, cloves, cinnamon stick, cilantro, tomatoes (with skin) and onion. Saute 10 minutes. The skin of tomatoes should blister some. Add chicken broth and chipotle taco seasoning and cook 10 minutes. Set aside to cool. Using a hand-held immersion blender or stand blender, blend the mixture. Add corn, chocolate, pumpkin seeds and almonds; blend until smooth. Return to heat and simmer 1 hour, stirring often to keep mixture smooth. Keep warm. Cut chicken strips into medium cubes. Rub with salt and black pepper and fully cook in a little water and oil. Serve as a fondue, using short bamboo skewers to dip chicken into mole sauce.

Steven Keith, "The Food Guy"
columnist for the Charleston Daily Mail

Baked Chicken with Peaches

8 skinless, boneless chicken
  breast halves
1 cup brown sugar, divided
4 fresh peaches, peeled, pitted
  and sliced

⅛ teaspoon ground ginger
⅛ teaspoon ground cloves
2 tablespoons fresh lemon
  juice

Preheat oven to 350°. Lightly grease a 9x13-inch baking dish. Place chicken in prepared baking dish and sprinkle with ½ cup brown sugar. Place peach slices over chicken, then sprinkle with remaining ½ cup brown sugar, ginger, cloves and lemon juice. Bake 30 minutes, basting often with juices, until chicken is cooked through and juices run clear.

Apple Chicken Stir Fry

1 pound cubed boneless,
  skinless chicken breast
1½ tablespoons vegetable oil,
  divided
½ cup onion, vertically sliced
  into slivers
1 cup thinly sliced carrots

1 teaspoon crushed dried basil
1 cup fresh or frozen Chinese
  pea pods
1 tablespoon water
1 medium apple, cored and
  thinly sliced
2 cups cooked rice

Stir-fry cubed chicken breast in 1 tablespoon vegetable oil in nonstick skillet until lightly browned and cooked. Remove from skillet and keep warm. Stir-fry onion, carrots and basil in remaining oil in same skillet until carrots are tender. Stir in pea pods and water; stir-fry 2 minutes. Remove from heat; stir in apple and chicken. Serve hot over cooked rice.

Linda McKay, West Virginia

Clementine Chicken

5 clementines
2 tablespoons soy sauce
1 teaspoon rice vinegar or
   white wine vinegar
1 teaspoon sesame oil
1 teaspoon brown sugar
¼ teaspoon ground ginger
½ tablespoon cornstarch
2 tablespoons vegetable oil

2 garlic cloves, peeled and
   minced
⅛ teaspoon crushed red
   pepper flakes
1 pound boneless, skinless
   chicken tenders, cut
   crosswise in half
4 green onions, thinly sliced

Peel 2 clementines and divide into segments. Set aside. Juice remaining clementines to yield ⅓ cup juice. Add soy sauce, vinegar, sesame oil, brown sugar, ginger and cornstarch; stir to combine well. Set aside. Heat vegetable oil in a large skillet or wok over medium-high heat. Add garlic and crushed red pepper flakes. Stir-fry 30 seconds. Add chicken and stir-fry 4 to 5 minutes until chicken is no longer pink and starts to brown. Stir juice mixture and pour into skillet. Cook, stirring constantly, until sauce is thick and bubbly, about 1 minute. Remove from heat and stir in clementine segments. Scatter sliced green onions over top and serve with soba noodles or steamed rice. Makes 4 servings.

Spicy Almond Chicken

3 tablespoons butter
1 (3-pound) chicken, cut into
   pieces
1 (14-ounce) jar red currant jelly
½ cup yellow mustard
½ cup blanched slivered
   almonds
3 tablespoons brown sugar
2 tablespoons lemon juice
½ teaspoon ground cinnamon

Melt butter in a large skillet over medium heat. Add chicken and sauté 10 minutes or until lightly browned on all sides. Remove chicken from skillet and place in a 9x13-inch baking dish. Set aside.

Preheat oven to 350°. Add jelly, mustard, almonds, sugar, lemon juice and cinnamon to the skillet. Stir together and cook over medium heat, stirring constantly, until jelly dissolves. Pour mixture over chicken. Cover and bake 30 minutes. Remove cover and bake an additional 10 minutes or until chicken is cooked through and no longer pink inside.

Beer Battered Asian Chicken Strips

1 large egg
¼ cup hoisin sauce
¾ cup beer
1 cup all-purpose flour
1 teaspoon baking soda

Salt and pepper
Chicken strips or chicken
   breast chunks
Vegetable oil for frying

In a bowl, beat egg lightly with a whisk. Add hoisin sauce and beer. Add dry flour, baking soda and salt; mix until smooth. Cover and let stand 25 to 30 minutes to rise slightly. Dip each piece of chicken into batter and gently place into a skillet with hot oil. Cook and turn as needed to cook evenly until golden. Cook in batches to prevent lowering temperature of oil. Each tender should take about 6 to 8 minutes to cook. Drain on paper towels for a few minutes. Serve strips with additional hoisin sauce or sweet and sour sauce.

Tommy Atwater & Family, West Virginia

Easy Slow Cooker Chicken

2 pounds chicken tenders
1 cup pineapple juice
½ cup brown sugar
⅓ cup soy sauce
¼ cup chopped onion
¼ cup chopped bell pepper

Combine everything in a slow cooker. Stir to coat chicken. Cook on low for 6 to 8 hours. Serve over steamed rice, or with mixed vegetables or Asian-style vegetables.

Ginny Covington, Marshall

Baked Onion-Dip Chicken Quarters

4 chicken leg quarters
¼ cup butter or margarine, melted
1 (1-ounce) envelope dry onion soup mix

In the mid '70s, my mom used onion soup mix in just about everything we ate. Her recipe for Baked Onion-Dip Chicken Quarters was a standard dish I cooked often in my first apartment.

Spray a 9x13-inch glass baking dish with nonstick spray. Place chicken in dish and brush with melted butter. Sprinkle each piece evenly with dry onion soup mix. Refrigerate 30 minutes or longer so seasonings can soak into chicken. Bake in a 350° preheated oven for 30 to 40 minutes or until chicken is no longer pink and juices run clear.

Nolan Hibbler, WVU

Blues Brews & BBQ Festival

Snowshoe • First Weekend in August

Take the best craft brewers in West Virginia and combine them with great food, live music and amazing vistas from the top of the mountain and you get the Blues Brews & BBQ Festival. It just doesn't get much better than that.

304-572-5892 • www.snowshoemtn.com

Easy Slow Cooker BBQ & Onion Pulled Chicken

2 pounds skinless chicken breasts or
    tenders
½ sweet onion, chopped
1 cup barbecue sauce
½ cup prepared mustard
1 tablespoon minced garlic
Dashes chili powder
Dashes liquid smoke

Place everything in a slow cooker and cover. Cook on high 2 hours. Check and if there is excess liquid after 2 hours, place cover back on at an angle to allow some of the liquid to cook off for the last hour. But be careful that it does not dry out; place cover tightly on for last hour if needed. When chicken is done, break it up with a fork into pulled or shredded pieces. Serve hot, slightly drained if desired, on a bun or toasted Texas toast.

Ginny Covington, Marshall

Spicy Chicken Wing Marinade

4 tablespoons sesame oil
4 tablespoons white wine vinegar
3 tablespoons crunchy peanut
  butter

3 tablespoons clear honey
2 tablespoons chili sauce
2 pounds chicken wings

Whisk together marinade ingredients. Place chicken wings in a large container and pour over marinade, cover and refrigerate for as long as possible, preferably overnight. Preheat oven to 425° and bake chicken wings with marinade 35 to 45 minutes, turning and basting frequently.

West Virginia Beekeepers Association

Tried & True Wing Sauce

1 (12-ounce) bottle Franks
  Red Hot Sauce
1 stick (½ cup) butter
1 heaping tablespoon minced garlic
2 teaspoons cayenne pepper
  or to taste
1 tablespoon brown sugar
Salt and black pepper

I'm a lifelong Huntington resident and bleed green—except when they play my alma mater, Auburn! Regardless of where you cook wings or where your tailgate is, my tried and true wing sauce is a must.

Bring all ingredients to boil and simmer 10 to 15 minutes or until the sauce thickens.

Pryce M. Haynes III, Huntington, West Virginia

West Virginia Hot & Honey Chicken Wings

7 chicken wings
¾ cup picante sauce
⅔ cup honey
⅓ cup soy sauce
¼ cup Dijon-style mustard
3 tablespoons vegetable oil
2 tablespoons finely shredded
  fresh ginger
1½ teaspoons finely shredded
  orange peel

Cut off and discard wing tips; cut each wing in half at joint. Place in 9x13-inch baking dish. Combine remaining ingredients; mix well. Pour over chicken wings. Cover and refrigerate at least 6 hours or overnight. Place chicken wings and sauce in a single layer on foil-lined 10x15-inch jelly-roll pan. Bake at 400° for 40 to 45 minutes or until well browned. Serve warm or at room temperature with additional picante sauce. Recipe can be doubled.

West Virginia Beekeepers Association

Chicken Divan

2 (10-ounce) packages chopped broccoli, cooked and drained
3 or 4 stewed chicken breasts, cubed
2 (10-ounce) cans cream of chicken soup
¼ cup mayonnaise
1 teaspoon lemon juice
¼ teaspoon curry powder
¼ cup diced onion
1½ cups shredded medium Cheddar cheese, divided
½ cup seasoned stuffing mix
1 teaspoon melted butter

Place broccoli on bottom of a 9x13-inch baking dish. Layer cooked chicken over broccoli. Mix soup, mayonnaise, lemon juice, curry powder, onion and ¾ cup cheese; pour over chicken. Sprinkle remaining cheese over top. Combine stuffing mix and butter; sprinkle on top. Bake at 350° for 35 minutes.

Bill Lilly, Lilly and Line Families,
Jumping Branch

Baked Yogurt Chicken Tenders

½ cup non-fat plain yogurt
¼ cup water
Salt and pepper to taste
Italian seasoning
2½ pounds boneless chicken tenders or chicken breasts
2 cups Italian seasoned breadcrumbs
Grated Parmesan cheese
1 (15-ounce) can Italian-flavored tomato sauce
Shredded mozzarella cheese

Preheat oven to 400°. Combine yogurt, water, salt, pepper and Italian seasoning to taste in a large bowl. Add chicken tenders and gently turn until chicken is evenly coated. Combine breadcrumbs, Parmesan to taste and Italian seasoning to taste in a zip-close bag. Add a few tenders at a time, seal and shake until coated evenly. Place in a single layer on a treated or nonstick baking sheet with sides, leaving space between each tender. Repeat until all chicken is coated. Bake 15 minutes until tenders are just done; juices will run clear. Carefully coat each tender with a small amount of tomato sauce and top with mozzarella cheese. Cook an additional 5 minutes or until cheese is melted.

Hannah B. Turner, West Virginia

West Virginia Honey Mustard Chicken Pie

1 pound boneless, skinless
    chicken breast
¼ cup soy sauce
Oil for cooking
¼ cup finely chopped onion
1 clove garlic, minced
1 cup chicken broth
1 cup carrots, cut into
    matchsticks

4 to 6 tablespoons honey
1 heaping tablespoon
    prepared Dijon mustard
¼ cup chopped parsley
Salt and ground black pepper
    to taste
1 to 2 tablespoons cornstarch
1 (9-inch) double pie crust

Cut chicken into bite-size chunks and marinate in soy sauce. Pour enough oil in saucepan to coat bottom. Sauté onion and garlic over medium-high heat until onion is soft but not brown. Add chicken pieces and sauté until chicken is cooked through. Stir in chicken broth, carrots, honey, mustard, parsley, salt and pepper. Mix cornstarch with a few tablespoons cold water to make a paste. Bring chicken mixture to a boil and stir in cornstarch mixture. Cook, stirring constantly, until thick. Mixture should get pretty thick; add more cornstarch mixture if necessary. Line a pie pan with pie crust. Pour chicken mixture into pie shell. Top with second crust, sealing edges and cutting small slits in top to let steam escape. Bake at 425° for 15 minutes. Reduce heat to 350° and bake 30 minutes more or until crust is golden brown.

West Virginia Beekeepers Association

Annual Tomato Tasting Festival

Fairmont
Third Sunday in August

The Annual Tomato Tasting Festival hosted by the Marion County Master Gardener Association is the 3rd Sunday each August at the High Gate Carriage House in Fairmont. You'll sample more than 60 varieties of tomatoes provided by local growers judged for the Biggest, Best Tasting and People's Choice. Step outside, for lunch or to leisurely stroll the historic coal baron's estate grounds to the Farmers Market, musical entertainment, gardening and food clinics, children's activities, and other educational and heritage displays—WV Extension demonstrations, honeybees, basket weaving, and butterfly tent. Free Admission. There is no entry fee for tomatoes.

304-816-1379
marion.ext.wvu.edu/
marion_county_master_gardeners

Ground Chicken & Black Bean Burgers

2 pounds ground chicken
1 (15-ounce) can black beans
½ cup finely minced onion
1 egg white
Salt and pepper
Seasoning of your choice (Italian, chili powder, barbecue rub, etc.)

Place ground chicken in a large bowl. Drain, rinse and gently break up beans with a fork. Add beans, onion and egg white; mix well. Season to taste with salt and pepper plus your desired seasoning. Form into patties of equal size, large for regular burgers or small patties for sliders. Bake in a 375° oven on a drip pan or cook on grill until done. Sliders work better on grill as larger burgers tend to break up, so turn only as needed if grilling.

Patricia Henderson,
Mountaineers Alumni

Ground Chicken and Spinach Meatballs with Cucumber Sauce

CUCUMBER SAUCE:

2 cups plain yogurt
⅔ cup cucumber, peeled and
    very finely chopped
2 tablespoons dried dill

½ tablespoon ground cumin
Dash ground coriander
2 tablespoons lemon juice
Salt and pepper

MEATBALLS:

1 (10-ounce) box frozen chopped
    spinach, defrosted and patted
    dry
¼ cup finely crumbled feta cheese
1 pound ground chicken
1 small white onion, very finely
    chopped

1 or 2 egg whites (1 if large, 2 if
    small or medium)
1½ tablespoons minced garlic
1 tablespoon salt-free seasoning
2 tablespoons finely grated
    Parmesan cheese, optional
2 tablespoons Italian breadcrumbs

Combine Cucumber Sauce ingredients in a food processor and mix until smooth; refrigerate. Preheat oven to 400°. Squeeze as much water from spinach as you can. Chop into small pieces. Combine spinach, feta cheese, chicken, onion, egg white, garlic, seasoning, Parmesan cheese and breadcrumbs in a bowl. Mix well and form into 15 to 20 meatballs of equal size. Bake on a nonstick baking sheet 12 to 15 minutes or until golden brown and cooked through. Serve meatballs drizzled with sauce or with sauce on the side.

Melinda White and Family

FISH & SEAFOOD

Trout Amandine,
page 153

Mountain Mini Trout Cakes

12 ounces trout, flaked, or your favorite seafood
¼ cup finely chopped celery
¼ cup finely chopped green onions or scallions
⅓ cup mayonnaise
1 egg, lightly beaten
2 teaspoons seafood seasoning
½ tablespoon Dijon mustard
½ teaspoon hot sauce
1¼ cups store-bought dried breadcrumbs plus more for coating

Preheat oven to 475°. If using frozen seafood be sure to thaw and pat dry with paper towels. In a large bowl, combine seafood with celery, green onions, mayonnaise, egg, seafood seasoning, Dijon mustard, hot sauce and breadcrumbs. Don't over stir as you don't want to make a mush. Shape mixture into cakes slightly smaller than a ping-pong ball. Slightly flatten and coat gently with extra crumbs. Place on a nonstick baking sheet or very lightly greased baking dish. Allow for a little bit of spreading as they cook. Bake 15 minutes and check to see if they are firm. Cook an additional 5 minutes if needed. Garnish with lemon wedges and serve hot with a spicy seafood sauce or tartar sauce.

Tommy Atwater & Family, West Virginia

Italian Dressing Trout

8 trout fillets
Old Bay seafood seasoning
½ (12-ounce) can favorite beer
⅔ cup Italian dressing

I've used West Virginia trout and fresh grouper fillets from fishing trips to the Gulf of Mexico to make this simple recipe.

Place fillets in a large baking dish. Sprinkle lightly with seafood seasoning. Mix beer and Italian dressing in a bowl. Thoroughly coat fillets, cover and chill 30 minutes. Bake in a 375° oven or grill using a fish basket until fish flakes evenly.

Lamar Taylor, West Virginia

Italian Brook Trout

1 (12-ounce) can beer
8 brook trout fillets
1 tablespoon basil
Salt and pepper to taste
1 teaspoon Old Bay seasoning
2 teaspoons garlic powder
2 tablespoons Italian dressing

The native West Virginia brook trout is perhaps the most sought-after trout by anglers in the state. It thrives in small, cold, spring-fed streams and is known for putting up an excellent fight for its size. The brook trout is olive with lighter sides and a reddish belly (in males) and is easily identified by the light-colored edges of the lower fins. The brook trout was adopted as the West Virginia State Fish on March 23, 1973.

Pour beer over fish. Add basil, salt, pepper, Old Bay and garlic powder. Stir in Italian dressing. Chill 20 minutes. Heat grill until beer sizzles when dripped on a grate. Cook trout until fish flakes with a fork.

West Virginia Division of Natural Resources, South Charleston

Campfire Trout

4 trout, cleaned and heads
   removed
Salt and pepper to taste
4 tablespoons butter, divided

1 medium green bell pepper,
   sliced
1 clove garlic, minced
   (optional)

Place each trout on a piece of aluminum foil. Season with salt and pepper, then stuff cavity with 1 tablespoon butter, green pepper and garlic. Roll trout tightly in foil, forming packets. Use additional foil to secure each packet to a metal toasting rod to use as a handle when removing fish from coals. Cover fish packets in red-hot, smoldering coals of your campfire and cook until fish is done, 7 to 10 minutes depending on heat of fire.

Barbecued Trout

½ cup soy sauce
2 tablespoons vegetable oil
1 teaspoon dried rosemary

⅔ cup ketchup
2 tablespoons lemon juice
6 (6-ounce) rainbow trout fillets

In a medium bowl, mix together soy sauce, vegetable oil, dried rosemary, ketchup and lemon juice. Place trout in a baking dish and pour marinade over fish. Refrigerate approximately 1 hour, turning trout once. Preheat an outdoor grill to medium-high and lightly oil grate. Drain excess marinade from fish into a small saucepan. Bring marinade to a boil and then remove from heat. Place trout on prepared grill. Cook approximately 5 minutes on each side, or until tender and easily flaked. Baste fish with boiled marinade while grilling.

West Virginia Italian Festival National Pasta Cookoff

Clarksburg
Weekend Before Labor Day

West Virginia Italian Festival National Pasta Cookoff is a full day of fun including tasting great pasta. Held in the covered area of Clarksburg's Jackson Square Event Facility in downtown Clarksburg, cooks of all ages, professional and amateur, vie for the best red sauce, best white sauce and People's Choice award. Other activities throughout the day include live music, silent auction, hot pepper eating contest, and more. Ahhhhh Pastaaaa! It doesn't get any better than this.

304-622-2157 • www.wvihf.com

Trout Amandine

2 (10-ounce) whole trout, pan-dressed
Salt and pepper to taste
¼ cup all-purpose flour
4 tablespoons butter, divided
½ cup blanched slivered almonds
2 tablespoons lemon juice
1 tablespoon chopped fresh parsley for
    garnish

Rinse and pat dry trout. Season inside and out with salt and pepper. Dredge trout in flour. Heat 2 tablespoons butter in large skillet over high heat until melted. Add trout and brown both sides. Lower heat to medium and cook 5 minutes on each side or until cooked through. Remove trout to a serving plate and keep warm. Wipe out pan and add remaining butter. Cook butter over medium heat until it just begins to brown. Add almonds and lightly brown them. Pour sauce over fish and sprinkle with lemon juice and parsley. Garnish with fresh lemon slices if desired.

Pub-Style Beer Battered Cod

1 bottle beer (not light beer)
2 cups all-purpose flour plus more for dredging
2 to 3 teaspoons seafood seasoning
Hot sauce, optional
1½ pounds boneless, skinless cod fillets, each about the size of
    your palm
Salt and pepper
Lemon juice
Hot oil for frying in a Dutch oven

Combine beer, 2 cups flour, seafood seasoning and a few drops hot sauce in a bowl. Mix well and set aside. Pat fish dry with a paper towel; sprinkle with salt and pepper and lemon juice to taste. Lightly dredge each piece in flour then dip in beer batter. Prep and cook only a few pieces at a time. Cook in hot oil until golden brown. Remove from oil and rest on a wire rack over paper towels for a few minutes. Serve hot with French fries, coleslaw and hush puppies, if desired.

Marv and Melanie Henderson, West Virginia

Beer Battered Crappie

1 tablespoon Old Bay seasoning
1½ cups flour
Cooking oil

12 ounces beer
3 pounds crappie fillets
Salt and pepper

Mix Old Bay seasoning with flour. Heat 4 inches cooking oil in a Dutch oven. Take 1 cup flour mixture and stir in beer. Season fish with salt and pepper then dredge in remaining flour mixture. Dip into beer-flour mixture. Place in heated oil and fry until fish floats.

West Virginia Division of Natural Resources,
South Charleston

Fillets in Lemon Butter

1 pound fish fillets
½ to 1 teaspoon salt
⅛ teaspoon pepper
½ cup butter
½ cup chopped parsley

1 tablespoon lemon juice
½ cup buttery-flavored cracker
  crumbs
½ teaspoon paprika

In an 8x12-inch microwave-safe dish arrange fillets with thickest areas to outside edges of dish. Sprinkle with salt and pepper. In a small bowl, microwave butter on high for 1 minute or until melted. Blend in parsley and lemon juice; pour over fish. Top with cracker crumbs, and sprinkle with paprika. Microwave on high 6 to 8 minutes or until fish flakes. Makes 4 servings.

West Virginia Division of Natural Resources,
South Charleston

Heavenly Baked Fish

Skinless fish fillets
Lemon juice
Salt and pepper (go light on
   the salt)
Hidden Valley Ranch Seasoning
   & Salad Dressing Mix
Mayonnaise
Toasted breadcrumbs

Arrange fillets in a single layer in a buttered baking dish. Squeeze fresh lemon juice on each fillet; season with salt and pepper. (If you are using frozen fillets this may be done while fillets are still frozen then place them in the refrigerator to thaw.) Sprinkle fillets with dressing mix. Spread about ¼ inch mayonnaise over each fillet, making sure entire surface is covered evenly. Sprinkle with breadcrumbs. Bake in preheated 350° oven 15 to 20 minutes. Fillets are done when they easily flake apart and the meat is white.

West Virginia Division of Natural Resources,
South Charleston

You can use fresh West Virginia trout for this recipe or your choice of fish fillets including panfish and catfish or frozen white fish, grouper, and tilapia. Substitute Creole or Cajun seasoning for the ranch mix for a different twist.

Finish Line Fish

1 whole fish of your choice, 18 to 24
   inches long
2 lemons, 1 sliced and 1 halved
1 medium Vidalia onion, sliced
1 stick (½ cup) salted butter, sliced
Salt
Seafood seasoning

Scale fish. Remove entrails, head, tail and fins. Place fish on 3 large sheets of foil and fill body cavity with sliced lemon, sliced onion and sliced butter. Season to taste with salt and seafood seasoning. Carefully wrap fish in first sheet of foil, making as complete a seal as possible. Repeat with other sheets of foil, making as tight a seal as possible with each sheet. Place fish in your dishwasher either in a 9x13-inch baking pan or directly on top shelf. If you choose rack, make sure water won't penetrate foil. Start dishwasher on highest or Pots and Pans setting. At end of dishwasher cycle carefully take your dishwasher fish out, remove it from foil and place on a platter lined with lettuce leaves and cooked rice or risotto. Squeeze lemon halves over top of fish. Garnish with lemon zest or additional lemon slices and enjoy! Serves 2 to 6 people.

Dave Thomas, President, High Performance Heroes, Clarksburg,
www.hpheroes.org

As President of West Virginia-based High Performance Heroes, Dave Thomas is used to thinking outside the box. "We've pledged our time, talents, and resources to provide entry level exposure to wheel-to-wheel vintage road racing for our veterans that have been injured," Thomas said. "In order to accomplish this goal we, along with the generous support of the motorsports industry, development staff, and racing fans, modify and develop vintage small-bore racing cars to meet the specific needs of each of our drivers." That certainly requires out of the box thinking and so does Dave's Finish Line Fish, which is cooked entirely in your dishwasher!

Stuffed Creole Fish Pockets

Fish fillets, thawed if frozen, patted dry
Creole seasoning
Lemon juice
Pita bread, halved and opened
Tartar or remoulade sauce
Shredded lettuce
Chopped tomato
Sliced sweet onion

This is a very easy version of a po' boy sandwich using pita bread. Use any type of unbreaded, boneless white fish that you enjoy. The key is serving the sandwich while fish is still sizzling hot!

Lightly coat fish fillets with Creole seasoning and lemon juice. Bake on a cookie sheet at 350° until fish easily flakes. Place in pitas with sauce and toppings.

Andrew Moore, Charleston

Fish Stick Po' Boy Tacos

Frozen fish sticks
Tartar sauce
Thousand Island dressing
Wheat soft-shell taco shells
Shredded mixed salad greens
Chopped scallions
Chopped green bell pepper
Sliced tomatoes

This may not be a classic heirloom recipe, but it has fed a family of five on more than one occasion. We like to use fish sticks with as little breading as possible.

Cook fish sticks per package directions and chop into bite-size pieces. Mix 2 parts tartar sauce with 1 part Thousand Island dressing. Heat shells. Place fish in shells and top with toppings and sauce.

The Walker Family, Charleston

Fried Grouper with Roasted Red Pepper Aioli

2 pounds grouper fillets
Vegetable oil for frying
¼ cup milk
1 egg

¼ cup water
1½ teaspoons seafood seasoning
1½ cups self-rising flour
Salt and pepper to taste

ROASTED RED PEPPER AIOLI:

⅔ cup mayonnaise
⅓ cup finely chopped roasted
   red peppers
1½ tablespoons relish

2 teaspoons lemon juice
½ tablespoon hot sauce
½ teaspoon minced garlic

Pat fillets with a paper towel to remove excess moisture. If using catfish, cut out any dark-colored parts. Pour oil to a depth of 3 inches in a Dutch oven or to desired depth in a deep-fat fryer. Heat oil. Combine milk, egg, water and seafood seasoning in a large bowl. Place flour in a deep dish for dredging. Sprinkle fillets with salt and pepper and dredge in flour. Gently dip in milk mixture and then back into flour. Fry fillets in hot oil 3 minutes on each side or until golden brown. Don't cook too many at a time. Drain fillets on a wire rack over a cookie sheet lined with paper towels. Mix sauce ingredients in a bowl and serve with the fried grouper.

Melinda White

Deep-Fried Walleye Fillet

3 eggs
¼ cup milk
4 ounces saltine crackers
2 pounds walleye fillets

Salt and pepper to taste
Peanut oil for frying
2 fresh lemons, cut into wedges

Combine eggs and milk and beat until thoroughly mixed. Crush crackers in blender and place in separate dish. Season fillets with salt and pepper to taste. Dip in egg mixture then in cracker crumbs and deep-fry in peanut oil approximately 3 minutes on each side or until golden brown. Drain on paper towels and place on warm dish. Serve hot with lemon wedges. Delicious served with potato pancakes with applesauce. Makes 6 servings.

West Virginia Division of Natural Resources, South Charleston

Berkeley Springs International Water Tasting

Berkeley Springs
Last Full Weekend in February

More than 100 waters from around the USA and the planet compete for best tasting and packaging in this award-winning event that is the largest and longest-running water tasting in the world. The public can taste along and take home entries in the concluding Water Rush. A day-long water seminar brings experts from around the world to Berkley Springs for the annual Berkley Springs International Water Tasting. Free admission.

800-448-8797
www.berkeleysprings.com/water/about

Cornmeal Catfish and Chow-Chow Mayo Sauce

⅔ cup mayo
2 tablespoons chow-chow
1 tablespoon pickle relish
2 teaspoons seafood seasoning
2 cups cornmeal

½ cup flour
Salt and pepper
6 to 8 skinless, boneless catfish
   fillets
Vegetable oil for frying

Mix mayo, chow-chow, pickle relish and seafood seasoning. Chill until ready to serve. Mix cornmeal, flour, salt and pepper in a shallow pan and dredge catfish fillets in mix. Cook in hot oil until lightly golden. Serve hot with chow-chow sauce.

Lamar Taylor, West Virginia

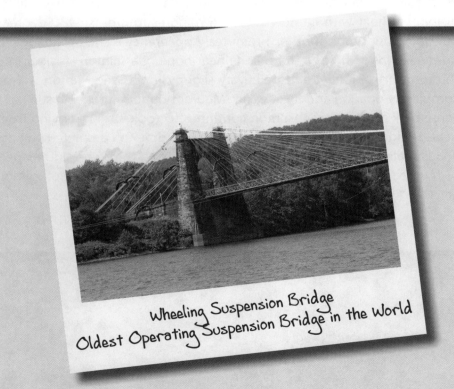

Wheeling Suspension Bridge
Oldest Operating Suspension Bridge in the World

Pryce's Tips for Cedar Plank Salmon

Fresh salmon steaks or fillets
Extra-virgin olive oil
Coarse salt and pepper
Herbs or salmon seasoning
Lemon

Grilled Salmon is an easy and delicious dish. Select the freshest salmon by watching for a bright orangey to red color and good texture. Soak the cedar plank at least an hour before preparing the recipe.

Lightly coat salmon with extra-virgin olive oil. Season with salt and pepper and herbs or seasonings of your choice. Drizzle with lemon juice. Place salmon skin side down on soaked cedar plank. Grill it over direct or indirect heat with lid down. After 5 minutes rotate fish 180 degrees but do not flip; cook another 5 minutes. Appearance is the best gauge of doneness. Insert tip of a sharp knife near bone of a salmon steak or into thickest part of a fillet and pull away slightly. Well-done salmon will be completely opaque and flake easily. Medium-done salmon will still have some pink at the center. Salmon continues to cook after removing from heat, so figure on 1 or 2 minutes of standing time to complete cooking. You can also judge proper cooking time by using the "Ten-Minutes-per-Inch Rule for Grilling, Broiling or Poaching." Measure the piece of salmon at its thickest part and cook 10 minutes for each inch of thickness.

Pryce M. Haynes III, Huntington

Pale Ale-Cedar Plank Salmon with Peach BBQ Sauce

Cedar planks
2 peaches, skinned and chopped
1 cup barbecue sauce
⅓ cup pale ale
1 tablespoon balsamic vinegar
2 or 3 tablespoons water
6 to 8 salmon fillets, each about the size of
    a deck of cards
Olive oil
Lemon juice
Salt and pepper to taste
Water

When cedar plank cooking, keep a water bucket nearby. Splash a little on any edges of the planks that may catch on fire, and dump the planks into the water to cool when cooking is complete.

Soak cedar planks in water. Place peaches in a saucepan. Break them up and mash with a fork. Add barbecue sauce, pale ale, vinegar and water. Bring to a boil and then reduce heat to low. Simmer and break up peaches a little more. Cook, stirring occasionally, until sauce slightly thickens. Remove from heat. Baste salmon with a little olive oil and sprinkle with lemon juice, salt and pepper. Place salmon on the cedar planks and cook on a grill over medium-high heat. Cook until flesh is opaque and flakes when tested with a fork. Remove salmon gently from planks, plate and top with a drizzle of sauce.

Nolan Hibbler, WVU

Tasty Honey Grilled Fish

¼ cup ThistleDew Farm honey
¼ cup chopped onion
2 tablespoons lime juice
2 tablespoons soy sauce
2 tablespoons hoisin sauce
2 cloves garlic, minced
1 jalapeño pepper, seeded and minced
1 teaspoon minced fresh ginger root
4 (4-ounce) swordfish steaks or firm white fish

Combine all ingredients except swordfish in small bowl; mix well. Place fish in shallow baking dish; pour marinade over fish. Cover and refrigerate 1 hour. Remove fish from marinade. Grill over medium-hot coals or broil 10 minutes per inch of thickness or until fish turns opaque and flakes easily when tested with fork.

Steve & Ellie Conlon, ThistleDew Farm, Proctor

Feast of the Seven Fishes

Fairmont
Second Saturday in December

One Saturday every December, thousands of people venture onto Monroe Street in downtown Fairmont for a fun day filled with authentic Italian cuisine, traditional holiday music, and unique gift shopping opportunities. This wildly anticipated event draws more than 8,000 visitors annually.

304.366.0468
www.mainstreetfairmont.org

Spaghetti with Anchovy, Garlic & Oil

1 pound thin pasta
1 tin anchovies
5 cloves garlic, minced
½ cup minced parsley and basil
Pepper and hot pepper flakes to taste
½ cup olive oil
½ cup reserved pasta water
½ cup grated Parmesan cheese

Bring a large pot of water to a rolling boil, add a generous pinch of salt, and cook pasta until al dente. Save ½ cup pasta water to incorporate into sauce. Drain pasta. In a skillet over medium-low heat, sauté anchovies, garlic, herbs, pepper and hot pepper flakes in olive oil about 5 minutes. Add reserved pasta water and cook until mixture thickens slightly. Toss spaghetti in anchovy sauce, top with Parmesan cheese, and enjoy.

Shannon Colaianni Tinnell
Feast of the Seven Fishes, Fairmont

Scapece

2 pounds smelt
Juice of 2 lemons
1 tablespoon salt
2 large onions, chopped
2 hot chilies
½ cup olive oil, divided
2 cups white wine or cider vinegar
10 sprigs fresh thyme
1 cup flour
1 tablespoon salt and pepper
1 head garlic, minced
1 teaspoon saffron threads

Scapece is a method of preserving fish, meat, and vegetables by first frying, then marinating in a vinegar bath. Other names include esabeche, escabecio, or seviche. Sardines may also be used in this recipe.

Clean smelt by splitting down the middle and pulling out the spine. Lay in a pan with lemon juice, salt, and enough water to cover bottom of pan. Leave smelt marinating in lemon water for about 30 minutes, turning once. Sauté onions and chilies in about 3 tablespoons olive oil until just starting to color around edges. Add vinegar and simmer until half the vinegar cooks away. Turn off heat and set aside. Add thyme and stir.

Pat smelt dry. Combine flour with 1 tablespoon each salt and pepper in a brown bag. Add smelt and shake to cover. Fry in remaining olive oil over medium-high heat and set aside to drain on a rack. Pour vinegar mixture over smelt; add garlic and saffron. Cover and store in a cool dark place overnight. It can also be left to marinate for up to a week. Serve with crusty Italian bread.

Shannon Colaianni Tinnell
Feast of the Seven Fishes, Fairmont

Shrimp Boil

12 small new potatoes
1 (16-ounce) package kielbasa sausage
8 ears fresh corn on cob
4 pounds medium-size shrimp

My husband, Martin Valeri, retired as General Superintendent of Olga Coal Company.

Bring large pot of water to boil. Add unpeeled potatoes and boil 10 minutes. Cut sausage into 3-inch pieces. Add to boiling water and boil 10 minutes. Add corn; boil 8 minutes. If using frozen corn boil only 5 minutes. Add washed shrimp; boil until shrimp turns pink. Serve with cocktail sauce, coleslaw and cornbread or garlic bread. Adjust amounts depending on number being served.

Marion Valeri, Coalwood Community United Methodist Church,
Cooking the Coalwood Way

West Virginia Sweet and Spicy Oven Shrimp

Seafood seasoning
Cajun or Creole seasoning
1 tablespoon minced garlic
2 to 3 tablespoons finely minced sweet
   onion
2 tablespoons fresh lemon juice
1 to 2 tablespoons honey
1 tablespoon soy sauce
¼ cup oil
1 pound large shrimp, shelled and
   deveined
Lemon wedges for garnish

Dad loved shrimp and my mom would come up with different ways to make it so we didn't always have the same thing over and over again. When I moved after college and would get homesick, I would tell people I was making West Virginia Shrimp. They would always look at me and wonder if West Virginia was near an ocean or something.

In a bowl, mix all ingredients except shrimp and lemon. (If shrimp is frozen, thaw and pat dry with a paper towel.) Add shrimp to marinade and gently toss to coat. Cover bowl and refrigerate an hour, stirring about halfway through. Preheat oven to 450°. Spread shrimp evenly in a medium-size baking dish or on a nonstick cookie sheet with sides. Bake 10 minutes and check for doneness. Garnish with lemon wedges and serve with seasoned rice, French bread, etc.

Lamar Taylor, West Virginia

CAKES

Sticky Bun Thump Cake (Monkey Bread), page 188

Apple Butter Cake

I grew up on apple butter and we used it for more than eating on a biscuit. My mom used apple butter in all kinds of dishes including this tasty cake.

1 (18-ounce) box spice cake mix
1 (21-ounce) can apple pie filling
3 eggs, lightly beaten
1 tablespoon butter, softened
⅓ cup plus 4 tablespoons apple butter, divided

CREAM CHEESE WALNUT ICING:

1 (8-ounce) package cream cheese, softened
1 cup powdered sugar
½ cup butter, softened
Chopped walnuts

In a large bowl combine cake mix with apple pie filling. Stir in eggs, butter and ⅓ cup apple butter. Bake in a greased and floured 9x13-inch pan at 350° for 30 minutes. Test with a toothpick. Don't over bake. Allow cake to cool before icing. In a bowl, combine icing ingredients except for walnuts. Use a hand-held mixer on low and beat very, very lightly until creamy. Mix in chopped walnuts as desired by hand using a spoon. Spread evenly over cake. You can also spread icing over cake and then sprinkle with chopped walnuts.

Andrew Moore, Charleston

Salem Apple Butter Festival

Salem
First Thursday thru Sunday of October

The Salem Apple Butter Festival provides live demonstrations of old-fashioned apple butter making. You will see the process done outdoors using copper kettles suspended over wood fire with the tasty product and canned on the spot for visitors to purchase. Other attractions include live entertainment, a grand parade, Saturday night fireworks, food, crafts, celebrity auction and many contests including apple pie baking, quilt show, the Sam Warner Memorial 5k Run, bicycle poker ride, pet show-off, talent show, car show, and horseshoe pitching and corn hole tournaments. The festival is a drug and alcohol free event providing family fun for all ages. There is no admission charge and all entertainment is free, as well.

304-782-1518
salemapplebutterfestival.com

Applesauce Cake

1 cup (2 sticks) butter, softened
2 cups sugar
1½ teaspoons baking soda
½ cup warm water
3 cups applesauce
4 beaten eggs
3½ cups flour

1 teaspoon baking powder
1 teaspoon cinnamon
1 teaspoon cloves
1 teaspoon nutmeg
1½ cups chopped nuts
½ pound raisins

Cream together sugar and butter. Dissolve baking soda in warm water and pour into applesauce. Stir into creamed mixture. Add eggs and beat well. Sift together flour, baking powder and spices; mix into wet ingredients. Add chopped nuts and raisins. Bake in a greased and floured 9x13-inch baking dish at 250° for 4 hours.

Guylinda Bailey, Coalwood
Coalwood Community United Methodist Church

Orange Cake

1 (15.25-ounce) box vanilla or golden (pudding in the mix) cake mix
4 eggs
½ cup oil
1 (11-ounce) can mandarin oranges
1 (16-ounce) can crushed pineapple, drained
1 (3.4 ounce) box vanilla instant pudding
1 (8-ounce) container Cool Whip

Mix cake mix, eggs, oil and mandarin oranges with juice according to box directions. Bake in 9x13-inch glass dish or pan at 350°. Let cool. Add pineapple and pudding mix to Cool Whip and mix well. Spread over top of cake and enjoy with a good cup of coffee.

Depression Raisin Cake

2 cups boxed raisins
1½ cups water
½ cup shortening
2 cups packed light brown sugar
3 cups all-purpose flour
1½ teaspoons cinnamon
½ teaspoon ground cloves
½ teaspoon nutmeg
½ teaspoon salt
1 cup milk
1 teaspoon baking soda
3 eggs, lightly beaten
Powdered sugar

My grandmother made raisin cake all the time. She called it Depression cake but my mom called it Ration Cake from WWII. The key is to pre-cook the raisins in water to soften and plump them up.

In a saucepan, combine raisins and water and cook over medium heat until soft and plump. Drain, reserving 2/3 cups raisin water; set aside. In a bowl, cream shortening with brown sugar. In another bowl, combine flour, cinnamon, cloves, nutmeg and salt; set aside. In a separate bowl, combine milk, soda, eggs and reserved raisin liquid. Combine all three mixtures and pour into a greased 9x13-inch baking pan and bake in a preheated 350° oven 30 to 35 minutes or until cake tests done with a toothpick. Allow to cool before slicing. Sprinkle with powdered sugar before serving.

Scott Williamson, West Virginia

West Virginia Hornets Nest Cake

1 (3-ounce) box cook-and-serve vanilla pudding
2 cups milk
1 (15.25-ounce) box Duncan Hines yellow cake mix
1 (12-ounce) package butterscotch chips
1 cup pecans, chopped

Combine pudding and milk in a microwave-safe container and microwave on high 6 minutes, stirring every 2 minutes. Add cake and stir; batter will be lumpy. Put into a greased and floured 9x13-inch pan. Press butterscotch chips and nuts lightly into top of cake. Bake at 350° for 30 to 35 minutes.

Bill Lilly, Lilly and Line Families, Jumping Branch

Sour Cream Sheet Cake

1 (18-ounce) box devil's food cake mix
½ cup sour cream (not low fat)
1 cup water
2 tablespoons cocoa powder
2 tablespoons vegetable oil
3 eggs
1 (16-ounce) can chocolate icing
¾ cup chopped pecans
¾ cup chocolate chips

Preheat oven to 350°. In a bowl, combine cake mix, sour cream, water, cocoa powder, vegetable oil and eggs. Spoon batter into a greased and floured 10x15-inch cake pan. (If you use spray nonstick spray, be sure to use the type with flour mixed in.) Bake 20 minutes or until a toothpick inserted in the center comes out clean. Cool. Top with icing, pecans and chocolate chips before slicing to serve.

Scott Williamson, West Virginia

Frosted Honey Cake

2 cups white whole-wheat flour, sifted
2 teaspoons baking powder
1½ teaspoons cinnamon
¼ teaspoon baking soda

¼ cup butter, softened
2 eggs
1 cup honey
1 teaspoon vanilla
⅔ cup 1% milk

HONEY FROSTING:
1 (8-ounce) package cream cheese, softened

¼ cup honey
½ teaspoon vanilla extract

Heat oven to 350°. Spray 2 (8-inch) cake pans with cooking spray and dust with all-purpose flour. Whisk together whole-wheat flour, baking powder, cinnamon and baking soda. In a stand mixer, cream butter on medium speed until light and fluffy. Add eggs 1 at a time, mixing well after each addition. Add honey and vanilla and beat until smooth. On low speed, add flour mixture alternately with milk, starting and ending with flour mixture, and mixing just until blended. Portion batter into prepared cake pans, dividing it evenly. Bake 20 to 25 minutes or until top of cakes spring back when lightly pressed. Cool in pans 15 minutes; unmold onto a rack and cool completely.

For the frosting, beat cream cheese, honey and vanilla until light and fluffy. Spread half the frosting onto 1 layer, place second layer on top and spread with remaining frosting. If frosting is too soft, refrigerate about 30 minutes or until frosting starts to firm up. Cut cake into 10 pieces to serve.

Marv and Melanie Henderson, West Virginia

Gluten-Friendly Honey Cake

½ cup brown rice flour*
½ cup garbanzo flour*
1 tablespoon baking powder
¼ cup brown sugar
⅛ teaspoon kosher salt
¼ teaspoon ground ginger
1 tablespoon orange zest

¼ cup orange blossom honey
1 teaspoon vanilla extract
1 egg
½ cup buttermilk
2 tablespoons butter, melted
¼ cup unsweetened applesauce

CRUMB TOPPING:

¾ cup gluten-free oats
2 tablespoons cold butter

2 tablespoons brown sugar
Honey, for drizzling

Preheat oven to 400°. In large bowl, whisk the flours, baking powder, sugar, salt, ginger and orange zest together. In separate bowl, whisk together honey, vanilla extract, egg, buttermilk, melted butter and applesauce. Combine with flour mixture and stir until just combined. For the topping, mix oats, cold butter and sugar until crumbly. Coat an 8x8-inch pan with butter or cooking spray. Pour cake batter into pan and top with crumb topping. Drizzle with honey. Bake 25 minutes or until toothpick inserted in center comes out clean.

*Note: May substitute ½ cup gluten-free all-purpose baking flour for each.

West Virginia Beekeepers Association

Neva's Hawaiian Cake

2 sticks (1 cup) margarine, softened
2 cups sugar
5 eggs
1 cup milk
1 cup shredded coconut
1 cup chopped nuts
1 cup crushed pineapple, drained
1 (13.5-ounce) box graham crackers, crushed into crumbs
2 teaspoons baking powder

PINEAPPLE ICING:

1 stick (½ cup) margarine, melted
1 cup crushed pineapple, well drained
1 (16-ounce) box powdered sugar

For the cake, cream butter and sugar. Add eggs and beat well. Blend in milk, coconut, nuts, pineapple, cracker crumbs and baking powder. Bake at 350° for 30 to 40 minutes or until done. For the icing, mix ingredients together and pour over cake while it is still warm.

Bill Lilly, Lilly and Line Families,
Jumping Branch

Hummingbird Cake

3 cups all-purpose flour
2 cups sugar
1 teaspoon salt
1 teaspoon baking soda
1 teaspoon ground cinnamon
3 eggs, beaten
1½ cups oil
1 (8-ounce) can crushed pineapple,
    undrained
2 cups chopped bananas
1 teaspoon vanilla
2 cups chopped pecans, divided

CREAM CHEESE FROSTING:

2 (8-ounce) packages cream cheese, softened
1 cup (2 sticks) butter or margarine, softened
2 (16-ounce) packages powdered sugar
2 teaspoons vanilla

For the cake, combine dry ingredients in a large bowl; add eggs and oil, stirring until dry ingredients are moistened. Do not beat. Stir in pineapple, bananas, vanilla and 1 cup pecans. Spoon batter into 3 well-greased and floured 9-inch cake pans. Bake at 350° for 25 to 30 minutes or until cake tests done. Cool 10 minutes. Remove from pans and cool completely. For the frosting, combine cream cheese and butter. Cream until smooth. Add powdered sugar and beat until light and fluffy. Add vanilla. Ice cake and sprinkle remaining pecans on top of frosting.

Avis Todd, Coalwood
Coalwood Community United Methodist Church

Chocolate Chocolate Angel Food Cake

12 large egg whites
1 teaspoon cream of tartar
1¼ cups sugar
¼ teaspoon salt
1 teaspoon vanilla extract

¾ cup cake flour, Presto-brand
   preferred
¼ cup cocoa powder
¼ cup chocolate syrup

Preheat oven to 325°. Beat egg whites in a large bowl for a few minutes before adding cream of tartar. Continue to beat until egg whites stand in stiff peaks. Sift sugar and salt together. (If using granulated sugar instead of superfine bar sugar, sift it twice.) Slowly add sugar to beaten egg whites along with vanilla. Continue beating until peaks are stiff and shiny. Sift flour and cocoa powder together and gently fold into mixture, taking care to deflate egg whites as little as possible.

Spoon a third of the batter into an ungreased angel food cake tin. Push mixture into and around sides of tin making sure there are no air bubbles. Drizzle half of the chocolate syrup over surface. Plunge a spoon or spatula about 3 times into batter for a marbled effect. Add another third of the batter and remaining chocolate syrup, plunging spoon into different areas than last time. Add remaining batter. Keep in mind that syrup will settle to bottom of tin during baking if you use too much or if it is all in one area.

Bake on middle or lower rack (so it doesn't brown too quickly) 50 to 60 minutes. Remove from oven and turn upside down on small feet on rim of tin to cool. It is important to cool cake upside down, otherwise it will be heavy. If your tin does not have feet, insert a narrow-neck bottle through hole in center of pan and invert it. Let it stay until completely cool. Run a serrated knife around inside and outside of tin to loosen. Also do same around bottom of tin once it has been removed from sides. Cut slices using a serrated knife in a sawing motion.

The Honorable & Mrs. John D. Rockefeller IV,
United States Senator, West Virginia

Easy Chocolate Cake

¾ cup all-purpose flour
⅔ cup sugar
½ cup unsweetened cocoa powder
1½ teaspoons baking powder
½ teaspoon salt
½ cup milk

3 tablespoons vegetable oil
⅔ cup packed brown sugar
¼ cup miniature semisweet
   chocolate chips
1 teaspoon vanilla extract
1¼ cups hot water

Preheat oven to 350°. Combine flour, sugar, cocoa, baking powder and salt in an 8x8-inch square pan. Stir in milk and oil; mix well. Set aside for 2 minutes then sprinkle with brown sugar and chocolate chips. In a small bowl combine vanilla and hot water. Gently pour over top of cake and set aside for 2 minutes to settle (do not stir). Bake 30 to 35 minutes until surface appears dry. Serve warm with a spoon or at room temperature.

Dr. Theresa Regan, West Virginia

This recipe is for one of the easiest cakes I've ever made came from a recipe swap. Be sure and preheat the oven before you start because the prep work only takes a few minutes.

Sourdough Chocolate Cake

1¾ cups all-purpose flour
⅔ cup unsweetened cocoa powder
¾ teaspoon baking soda
½ teaspoon baking powder
1 teaspoon salt
⅔ cup vegetable oil
1⅔ cups sugar
3 eggs
1 cup sourdough starter (see page 32)
1 cup buttermilk
1 teaspoon vanilla extract

Sift together flour, cocoa, baking soda, baking powder and salt. Cream together oil, sugar and eggs. Blend in sourdough starter. Add sifted ingredients slowly to creamed mixture, beating until smooth. Stir in buttermilk and vanilla and mix well. Pour into greased and floured 9x13-inch baking dish or Bundt pan and bake at 350° for 35 minutes or until cake tests done. When completely cool, sprinkle with powdered sugar, garnish with almonds or frost as desired.

Mary Jones, Kenna

Lewisburg Chocolate Festival

Lewisburg
Second Weekend in April

The Lewisburg Chocolate Festival is a chocolate lover's dream. This fun festival offers something for the whole family with a chocolate tasting extravaganza, live performances, chocolate mousse eating contest, bake-offs and professional demonstrations.

304-645-1000
www.lewisburgchocolatefestival.com

Biscuit-Mix Chocolate Cake

1 (16-ounce) package biscuit mix
2 cups sugar
½ cup (1 stick) butter
⅔ cup water
⅓ cup brewed coffee

¼ cup unsweetened cocoa powder
½ cup buttermilk
2 eggs
1 teaspoon vanilla

CHOCOLATE FROSTING:

½ cup (1 stick) butter
2 tablespoons unsweetened
    cocoa powder

¼ cup milk
3½ cups powdered sugar
1 tablespoon vanilla

Preheat oven to 400°. Combine biscuit mix and sugar in a bowl. In a saucepan, bring butter, water, coffee and cocoa to a boil while stirring. Pour over biscuit mixture and add buttermilk, eggs and vanilla. Mix well and pour into a greased and floured 9x13-inch baking dish. Bake 20 to 25 minutes. Cool before frosting. To make the frosting, in a saucepan combine butter, cocoa powder and milk. Heat to boiling. Mix in powdered sugar and vanilla until smooth using hand mixer on low. Spread over cake.

Marv and Melanie Henderson, West Virginia

Chocolate Sheet Cake

This sheet cake is very moist and easy to make. Cut and serve straight from the pan with a scoop of vanilla ice cream.

2 cups all-purpose flour
2 cups sugar
1 teaspoon baking soda
½ teaspoon salt
1 cup (2 sticks) butter or
    margarine

4 tablespoons cocoa powder
1 cup water
½ cup buttermilk
2 eggs, lightly beaten
1 teaspoon vanilla

CHOCOLATE FUDGE FROSTING:

½ cup (1 stick) butter
6 tablespoons buttermilk
4 tablespoons cocoa powder

1 teaspoon vanilla extract
1 (16-ounce) box powdered sugar
1 cup chopped nuts

Stir together first 4 cake ingredients in mixing bowl. Melt butter in a saucepan. Add cocoa and water. Bring to boil and pour over dry ingredients. Stir in buttermilk, eggs and vanilla. Blend well. Pour into a greased and floured sheet cake pan and bake in a preheated 350° oven 20 to 25 minutes until done. Test by inserting a knife into center of pan. The knife should come out clean. Do not overcook. Remove cake from oven. Leave it in pan and frost immediately while still warm.

For the frosting, melt butter in a saucepan over medium heat. Add buttermilk and cocoa. Blend well. Stir in vanilla. Add powdered sugar and stir until well blended. Fold in nuts. Frost cake immediately. Serve warm or cold.

Hannah B. Turner, West Virginia

West Virginia 7-Up Cake

1 (18.25-ounce) box vanilla
   cake mix
1 (3.4-ounce) box lemon
   pudding mix
4 eggs

¾ cup oil
¾ cup 7-Up
2 teaspoons vanilla extract
1 cup white chocolate chips,
   optional

Combine cake mix add lemon pudding mix in a large bowl. Add eggs, beating well after each addition. Add oil, 7-Up and vanilla extract. Stir to combine. Add white chocolate, if desired. Pour into a nonstick Bundt pan and bake in a preheated 325° oven 40 to 45 minutes.

Hannah B. Turner, West Virginia

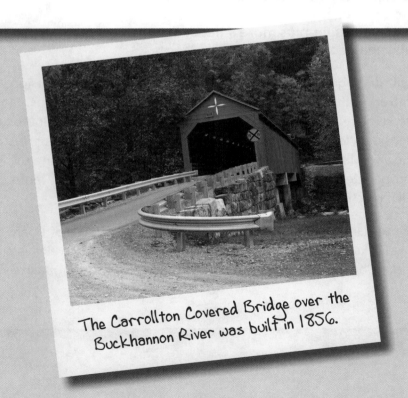

The Carrollton Covered Bridge over the Buckhannon River was built in 1856.

Sue Terry's Carrot Cake

CARROT CAKE:

2 cups flour
2 cups sugar
2 teaspoons baking soda
2 teaspoons salt
1¼ cups Wesson oil
4 eggs
3 cups grated carrots

CREAM CHEESE FROSTING:

1½ (8-ounce) packages cream cheese, softened
1 stick (½ cup) margarine or butter, softened
1 tablespoon vanilla
1 cup powdered sugar plus more if needed
¾ cup chopped pecans, optional

For cake, sift dry ingredients together. Add oil and eggs. Mix well, using low speed on your mixer. Fold in carrots. Pour into 2 greased round cake pans. Tap them on counter to remove bubbles. Bake in preheated 350° oven 35 minutes or until a tester comes out clean. Cool and ice with cream cheese frosting. For frosting, using electric mixer on low, blend softened cream cheese and margarine together with vanilla and powdered sugar until fluffy. If not stiff enough, add more powdered sugar until it reaches a nice frosting consistency.

Editor's Note: Linda mentions her husband, Homer Hickam, of Coalwood, West Virginia. Mr. Hickam is the author of the memoir *Rocket Boys* as well as several other novels. *Rocket Boys* was made into the movie *October Sky* starring Jake Gyllenhaal.

Linda Hickam

Lilly Family Black Walnut Carrot Cake

2 cups sugar
1 cup oil
4 eggs
½ teaspoon black walnut flavoring
1 teaspoon vanilla
2 cups self-rising flour
1 teaspoon cinnamon
3 cups ground carrots
1 cup black walnuts, chopped
1 cup crushed pineapple, drained

TOPPING:

1 cup sugar
1 teaspoon baking soda
½ cup buttermilk
1 tablespoon white Karo syrup

For the cake, mix the sugar, oil and eggs. Add flavorings, flour, cinnamon, carrots, walnuts and pineapple. Mix well. Pour into a greased tube pan and bake at 350° about 1 hour. For the topping, bring ingredients to a boil and boil 5 minutes. Pour over cake while hot.

Bill Lilly, Lilly and Line Families,
Jumping Branch

Blackberry Cake

1½ cups sugar
½ cup butter or Crisco
5 eggs
2 cups flour
2 teaspoons baking soda
2 teaspoons cinnamon
2 teaspoons nutmeg
½ teaspoon cloves
½ cup buttermilk
2 cups blackberries

Cream sugar, butter and eggs. In a separate bowl, combine flour, baking soda, cinnamon, nutmeg and cloves. Add to creamed mixture with buttermilk; mix well. Carefully stir in blackberries. Bake in a greased and floured tube pan at 350° for 1 hour. Frost with caramel or vanilla icing.

Mountain-Style Blackberry Jam Cake

1 cup shortening
2 cups sugar
3 egg yolks, well beaten
1 cup blackberry jam
3 cups flour

½ teaspoon salt
1 teaspoon baking soda
1 teaspoon cinnamon
1 cup buttermilk
½ cup chopped walnuts, optional

Cream shortening and sugar. Add egg yolks and jam; mix well. Sift dry ingredients together; add alternately with buttermilk, beating smooth after each addition. Add chopped nuts, if desired. Bake in greased sheet pan 30 minutes at 350°. If your pan measures 9x13 inches, additional baking time may be needed. Cool and frost with caramel icing.

Dr. Theresa Regan, West Virginia

West Virginia Black Walnut Festival

Spencer
Second Thursday in October

For 60 years, The Black Walnut Festival has entertained the area with a family-centered festival that is great fun for people of all ages. Featuring food, music, arts and crafts, 4H exhibits, a carnival, kid's day parade, marching band competition and the Grand Parade on Saturday, you will not want to miss this four-day festival—one of West Virginia's best festivals.

304-927-1640 • www.wvbwf.com

Sticky Bun Thump Cake (Monkey Bread)

⅔ cup sugar
3 teaspoons cinnamon
4 (8-ounce) cans biscuits
10 tablespoons butter
1 cup brown sugar

I asked why this was called "Thump Cake" and was told that THUMP is the sound of the canned biscuits being opened when they are smacked against the countertop.

Preheat oven to 350° and grease Bundt cake pan or treat with nonstick spray. In a bowl, combine sugar and cinnamon. Cut biscuits into quarters. Add biscuit pieces to bowl with cinnamon and sugar and shake or stir to coat pieces evenly. Layer in Bundt pan. In a saucepan, bring butter and brown sugar to a boil over medium heat while stirring. As soon as it boils remove from heat and drizzle over biscuit pieces. Bake 35 to 45 minutes or until golden. Cool about 10 minutes before removing from pan. Pull apart and serve warm in small portions with a bit of whipped cream.

Nolan Hibbler, WVU

Betty's Pumpkin Cupcakes

This recipe, created by Betty Enslin, won first place at the West Virginia Pumpkin Festival and was included in West Virginia's 2008 What's Cooking *cookbook.*

⅔ cup shortening
2 eggs
¾ cup maple syrup
½ cup milk
1½ cups all-purpose flour
1¼ teaspoons baking powder
½ teaspoon salt
½ teaspoon baking soda

½ teaspoon ground ginger
½ teaspoon ground allspice
1 cup canned pumpkin
1 (8-ounce) can crushed
   pineapple, drained

FROSTING:
1 (8-ounce) package cream
   cheese, softened

¼ cup butter, softened
1½ cups powdered sugar

In large mixing bowl, beat shortening until light and fluffy. Add eggs, 1 at a time, beating well after each addition (mixture will appear curdled). Beat in syrup and milk. Combine flour, baking powder, salt, baking soda, ginger and allspice; add to shortening mixture and beat just until moistened. Stir in pumpkin and pineapple. Fill paper-lined muffin cups three quarters full. Bake at 350° for 20 to 25 minutes or until toothpick comes out clean. Cool 10 minutes before removing from pans to wire rack to cool completely. For frosting, in small mixing bowl beat cream cheese and butter until fluffy. Add powdered sugar; beat until smooth. Frost cupcakes. Yields 16 cupcakes.

West Virginia Department of Agriculture

Butternut Pound Cake

2 sticks (1 cup) butter, softened
½ cup Crisco
3 cups sugar
5 eggs
1 (10-ounce) jar maraschino
　　cherries with juice

3 cups all-purpose flour
1 (5-ounce) can evaporated milk
2 tablespoons butternut flavoring
Dash salt
1 cup chopped nuts

Cream butter and Crisco well. Add sugar, 1 cup at a time, beating well after each addition. Add eggs, 1 at a time, beating well after each addition. Add enough cherry juice to evaporated milk to make 1 cup. Alternate adding flour and evaporated milk to batter, mixing well after each addition. Add flavoring, salt and nuts. Chop drained cherries, add to batter and blend well. Place batter in a greased and floured pound cake pan or 2 loaf pans. Bake 1½ hours at 300° or until cake tests done.

Bill Lilly, Lilly and Line Families,
Jumping Branch

Sour Cream Bundt Cake

1 cup butter
2 cups plus 3 teaspoons sugar, divided
½ teaspoon vanilla
2 eggs
2½ cups sifted all-purpose flour
1 teaspoon baking powder
¼ teaspoon salt
2 teaspoons cinnamon, divided
1 cup chopped pecans
½ cup raisins
1 cup sour cream

In a large bowl, cream butter adding 2 cups sugar as you go. When creamed, stir in vanilla. Lightly beat 1 egg; mix into the batter. Repeat with second egg. In a separate bowl, sift together flour, baking powder, salt and 1 teaspoon cinnamon. Add nuts and raisins; stir. Alternate adding fold mixture and sour cream into creamed mixture. Pour batter into a greased and floured Bundt pan. Combine remaining 3 teaspoons sugar and 1 teaspoon cinnamon; sprinkle over cake. Bake in preheated 350° oven 50 minutes or until a toothpick inserted in center comes out clean. Cake should not bake more than an hour or the edges and bottom may burn. Let cake rest 1 hour before removing from pan. Loosen edges and turn out upside down onto a rack to finish cooling.

Julie DeMary, Monongah

Jackson's Mill Cornmeal Pound Cake

6 tablespoons butter
1 cup sugar
4 eggs
1¼ cups sifted pastry flour
¾ teaspoon baking powder
¼ cup sifted white cornmeal
⅛ teaspoon freshly grated
    nutmeg or ¼ teaspoon
    powdered nutmeg
¼ teaspoon cinnamon
2 teaspoons brandy, preferably
    apple brandy
½ teaspoon vanilla

Originally settled by Colonel Edward Jackson before 1800, the small town of Jackson's Mill boasted saw and grist mills, a carpenter shop, blacksmith forge, slave quarters, numerous barns/outbuildings, and a general store. Three generations of Jacksons operated variations of the mill at the site. Divided and passed through several hands over the years, the remaining property was deeded to West Virginia in 1921. Located near Weston, this historic area is maintained by West Virginia University. Today, all that remains of the original settlement are the gristmill and the Jackson family cemetery.

By hand or with an electric mixer, thoroughly cream butter and sugar until fluffy. Beat in eggs 1 at a time. Sift together flour, baking powder and cornmeal. Combine spices with flour mixture. Blend dry ingredients into the batter by hand, alternating with brandy and vanilla. Pour into greased round layer cake pan, an 8-inch square pan, or 10x6-inch pan that has been lined with greased wax paper. Bake at 325° for 1½ hours. Remove from oven and cool 10 minutes. Invert onto cake rack and strip off wax paper.

Jackson's Mill, Weston,
West Virginia University

COOKIES & CANDIES

Caramel Chocolate Chip Apples, page 211

Apple Butter Bars

½ cup butter
1½ cups all-purpose flour, divided
½ cup packed brown sugar
¼ cup granulated sugar
1 egg
¾ cup apple butter
½ teaspoon baking soda
½ teaspoon apple pie spice
1 cup raisins
1 cup powdered sugar
¼ teaspoon vanilla extract
1 to 2 tablespoons milk

Preheat oven to 350°. Grease a 9x13-inch baking pan. Beat butter until creamy. Add half the flour, the brown sugar, granulated sugar, egg, apple butter, baking soda and apple pie spice. Beat together until well blended. Beat in remaining flour and stir in raisins. Spread in prepared baking pan. Bake 20 to 25 minutes or till toothpick inserted in center comes out clean. Cool in pan on wire rack. For the icing, mix powdered sugar, vanilla and 1 to 2 tablespoons milk to make a drizzling consistency. Drizzle over pan and cut into bars.

West Virginia Apple Butter Cookies

¼ cup sugar
½ cup shortening
1 cup apple butter
1 teaspoon baking soda
2¼ cups flour

½ teaspoon salt
1 teaspoon baking powder
½ cup milk
½ teaspoon vanilla
½ cup chopped nuts

Preheat oven to 350° and grease a cookie sheet. In a bowl, cream sugar and shortening. Add apple butter and baking soda. Mix flour, salt and baking powder and add alternately with milk. Mix well. Add vanilla and nuts. Drop by teaspoon onto prepared cookie sheet. Bake 10 to 12 minutes.

Moist and Tasty Apple Cookies

2 cups peeled, chopped apples
1 cup strong coffee
1 cup sugar
1 cup raisins
½ cup butter, softened
1 teaspoon ground cinnamon
¾ teaspoon ground nutmeg

¾ teaspoon ground cloves
2 cups all-purpose flour
¼ teaspoon salt
1 teaspoon baking soda
1 teaspoon vanilla extract
1 cup chopped nuts

Combine first 8 Ingredients in a saucepan; cook over low heat until apples are tender. Remove from heat; cool. Combine flour, salt and soda; stir into apple mixture. Add vanilla and nuts, stirring well. Drop by teaspoonfuls onto ungreased cookie sheet. Bake at 375° for 15 minutes. Makes about 4½ dozen cookies.

West Virginia Department of Agriculture

Dandelion Cookies

A great cookie to make with children.

½ cup vegetable oil
½ cup honey
2 eggs, beaten
1 teaspoon vanilla
1 cup whole wheat flour
1 cup oats
¼ cup dandelion petals (remove yellow flower petals from green; use petals only)
¼ cup sunflower seeds

In a medium-sized bowl, stir together oil and honey. Stir in eggs and vanilla. Add flour, oats and flower petals. Drop onto greased cookie sheet. Sprinkle sunflower seeds on each cookie. Bake at 375° for 6 to 7 minutes.

M. Dawson, Buckeye
Wild Edibles Festival

Wild Edibles Festival
Buckeye
Third Saturday in April

Get a taste of Pocahontas County at the annual Wild Edibles Festival. Choose from a variety of workshops and walks where you will learn where to gather, how to identify, and how to prepare the delicious bounty of wild edible plants. Make and sample wildflower teas, main dishes, and desserts made with greens and flowers you won't find at the supermarket. There is silent auction and vendors for your enjoyment.

304-799-4636
www.pocahontascountywv.com

Pumpkin Cookies

1 cup Crisco
1 cup sugar
1 cup pumpkin purée
1 egg
1 teaspoon vanilla
2 cups flour

1 teaspoon baking powder
1 teaspoon baking soda
1 teaspoon cinnamon
½ teaspoon salt
½ cup chopped nuts, optional
½ cup raisins, optional

ICING:

3 tablespoons butter
4 tablespoons milk
½ cup brown sugar

1 cup powdered sugar
½ teaspoon vanilla

Cream together Crisco and sugar. Add pumpkin, egg and vanilla. Sift together flour, baking powder, baking soda, cinnamon and salt; add to creamed mixture. Stir in optional ingredients if using. Drop by teaspoons onto ungreased cookie sheets. Bake at 350° for 15 minutes. For the icing, place butter, milk and sugar in a saucepan. Bring to a boil and boil 2 minutes. Cool and add powdered sugar and vanilla. Beat with spoon until spreadable.

Linda Boggess and Kay Solomon,
St. Albans Historical Society, St. Albans

Honey Peanut Butter Oatmeal Cookies

1 cup butter
½ cup granulated sugar
1 cup peanut butter
¼ cup brown sugar
2 eggs
1 teaspoon vanilla
½ cup honey
1½ cups flour
1 teaspoon salt
1¼ teaspoons baking soda
2½ cups quick oatmeal

This recipe came from a tag attached to honey that I bought from a local produce market outside Charleston. I wish I still had the name of the honey because it was local to the area and very delicious.

Combine butter, granulated sugar, peanut butter and brown sugar until creamy. Add eggs and vanilla; mix well. Mix in honey and beat until fluffy. In a separate bowl, sift flour with salt and baking soda; add to creamed mixture. Gently stir in oatmeal. Drop spoonfuls onto ungreased cookie sheet. Bake at 325° for 10 to 12 minutes.

Hannah B. Turner, West Virginia

Peanut Butter & Honey Cookies

½ cup shortening
1 cup honey
½ cup peanut butter
1 egg
½ teaspoon salt
1¼ cups flour
½ teaspoon soda

Cream shortening, honey and peanut butter. Add egg and beat until light and fluffy. Sift dry ingredients together and stir into creamed mixture. Drop by teaspoons onto a lightly greased cookie sheet. Bake 12 to 15 minutes at 325°.

West Virginia Department of Agriculture

Oatmeal Chews

½ cup butter
¾ cup honey
1 egg
1 teaspoon vanilla
⅔ cup sifted flour
½ teaspoon baking soda
½ teaspoon baking powder
¼ teaspoon salt
1 cup quick-cooking rolled oats
1 cup flaked coconut
½ cup chopped almonds

Cream butter and honey until light and fluffy. Add egg and vanilla; beat well. Sift together flour, baking soda, baking powder and salt. Add to creamed mixture. Stir in oatmeal, coconut and almonds. Spread in greased 9x13-inch baking pan. Bake at 350° for 20 to 25 minutes. When cool, cut into bars. Makes 30.

West Virginia Department of Agriculture

Molasses Sugar Cookies

¾ cup shortening
1 cup sugar plus more for topping
1 egg
¼ cup molasses
2 cups all-purpose flour
½ teaspoon salt
1½ teaspoons baking soda
1 teaspoon cinnamon
½ teaspoon ginger
½ to 1 teaspoon cloves

Cream shortening with an electric mixer. Gradually add 1 cup sugar, beating until light and fluffy. Add egg and molasses; mix well. Combine flour, salt, soda and spices; mix well. Add a quarter of the dry mixture at a time to creamed mixture, mixing until smooth after each addition. Chill 1 hour. Roll dough into 1-inch balls. Roll in sugar. Place 2 inches apart on ungreased cookie sheet. Bake at 375° for 10 minutes. Tops will crack. Makes 4½ dozen.

Mary Jane Robinson and Verda Bush
Molasses Festival

CALHOUN CHRONICLE NEWSPAPER - BILL BAILEY

West Virginia Molasses Festival
Arnoldsburg
Last Full Weekend in September

For more than 40 years the West Virginia Molasses Festival has supported the West Fork Community Action which was organized in 1965 for the purpose of developing a community center. The committee depended on raising cane and processing it into sorghum molasses to pay the loan on the land. When a second loan was needed for a building, the Festival was born. This fun, 3-day festival features exhibits, country store items, molasses making demonstrations, a pageant, food vendors, arts & craft vendors, sausage and pancake supper, cake walks, gospel music, a parade, children's games, a greased pig contest and more. Join us for history, heritage and lots of fun.

304-655-7371

Molasses Raisin Cookies

3¼ cups all-purpose flour
1 teaspoon baking soda
¼ teaspoon salt
2 teaspoons ground cinnamon
1 teaspoon ground ginger
½ teaspoon allspice

1 cup packed dark brown sugar
1 cup salted butter
1 cup unsulfured molasses
1 large egg
1½ cups (6 ounces) raisins

Preheat oven to 300°. In a medium bowl, combine flour, soda, salt, cinnamon, ginger and allspice. Mix well with a wire whisk and set aside. In a large bowl, beat sugar and butter with an electric mixer at medium speed until mixture forms a grainy paste. Scrape sides of bowl then add molasses and egg. Beat until light and fluffy. Add flour mixture and raisins; blend at low speed just until combined. Do not over mix. Divide dough in half and shape each half into a roll 1½ inches in diameter. Wrap rolls in waxed paper and refrigerate until firm, about 2 hours. Slice cookies ½ inch thick and place on ungreased cookie sheets, 1½ inches apart. Bake 25 to 27 minutes or until cookies are set. Immediately transfer cookies with a spatula to a cool surface. Makes 4 dozen cookies.

ICING:

1 cup powdered sugar

2 tablespoons milk

Blend sugar and milk in a small bowl until smooth. Using a small spoon or knife, drizzle cookies with icing.

West Fork Community Action
Molasses Festival

Cast-Iron Skillet Chocolate Chip Cookie

6 tablespoons unsalted butter, softened
½ cup granulated sugar
⅓ cup packed dark brown sugar
1 large egg
1 teaspoon vanilla extract

1 cup all-purpose flour
½ teaspoon baking soda
½ teaspoon coarse salt
1 cup semisweet chocolate chips
1 cup finely chopped pecans, optional

Preheat oven to 350°. Combine butter, granulated sugar and brown sugar with a spoon or electric mixer on medium speed. Mix until light and fluffy. Mix in egg and vanilla. Stir in flour, baking soda and salt. Stir in chocolate chips and nuts. Spoon dough into 4 or 5 mini cast-iron skillets or 1 (10-inch) cast-iron skillet. Spread dough evenly and smooth top with a moist spoon. Bake at 350° for 18 to 20 minutes depending on size of your skillet; times will vary. Bake until golden brown and firmed up in the middle. Allow cookie to cool and serve plain or topped with icing like you would a cake.

Scott Williamson, West Virginia

Brownie Truffles

For variety, use mini chocolate chips, multi-colored sprinkles, or chocolate sprinkles instead of powdered sugar to coat the truffles.

1 box low-fat fudge brownie mix
½ cup water
1 egg
1 cup chocolate chips
1 cup powdered sugar

Preheat oven to 350°. Combine brownie mix, water, egg and chocolate chips. Pour into 9x13-inch glass pan and bake 20 minutes. Brownies will be soft. Cool 10 minutes. Using a melon baller, shape brownies into 1-inch balls. Place powdered sugar in zip-close bag. Drop balls into bag of sugar and coat. Makes 24 truffles.

No Bake Coconut Chocolate Patties

2 cups sugar
¼ cup cocoa
½ cup milk
½ cup butter
1 cup crunchy peanut butter
1 teaspoon vanilla
2 cups quick rolled oats
1 cup coconut

Lightly grease 9x13-inch pan. In large saucepan, combine sugar, cocoa, milk and butter. Bring to a boil over medium heat, stirring constantly. Remove from heat as soon as it comes to a boil. Add peanut butter and vanilla; mix well. Stir in oats and coconut. Pour into prepared pan; cover and refrigerate. Cut into bars. Store in refrigerator.

The Walker Family, Charleston

West Virginia Chocolate Festival
Ripley
Day Before Palm Sunday

The West Virginia Chocolate Festival is all things chocolate. From truffles to molded suckers, from dipped fruit to fudge, chocolate bunnies to chocolate covered popcorn. If it is made with chocolate, we probably have it. This is a family event with free admission and free parking.

304-531-1133

Hot Chocolate Potato Chip Candy

VERSION ONE:

1 package chocolate bark for candy making
2 or 3 teaspoons hot sauce
1 (10-ounce) bag potato chips, wavy or thick style

Melt chocolate as per instructions on package. Stir in hot sauce, but don't use too much as it may thin chocolate coating too much. Dip each chip halfway into chocolate and place on wax paper to set.

VERSION TWO:

1 package chocolate bark for candy making
2 or 3 teaspoons hot sauce
1 (10-ounce) bag potato chips, crumbled but not too small

Melt chocolate as per instructions on package. Stir in hot sauce, but don't use too much as it may thin chocolate coating too much. While chocolate is still liquid, stir in potato chip pieces. Gently mix with a spoon. Spoon equal portions about the size of a quarter or smaller onto a wax paper-lined cookie sheet.

Barney Gullatt, West Virginia Mountaineers

Peanut Butter Cookie Candy Bars

2 sticks margarine, softened
1 cup peanut butter
1 (16-ounce) box powdered sugar
1½ cups graham cracker crumbs
1 (16-ounce) bag milk chocolate chips

I sometimes coat the finished bars with white chocolate candy coating for variety.

In a large bowl, cream together margarine, peanut butter, powdered sugar and graham cracker crumbs. Mix well and spoon into the bottom of a 9x13-inch dish treated with nonstick spray. Melt chocolate chips in microwave or over hot water, as directed. Spread chocolate over peanut butter layer. Let chocolate set before cutting into bars.

Kimmie Morgan, West Virginia

Becka's Fruit Loop Candy

20 ounces almond bark
2 cups colored mini marshmallows
1 cup shelled, skinned salted
   peanuts
1 cup chopped pecans or walnuts
2 cups rice crisp cereal
2 cups fruit loop cereal

Melt almond bark in microwave according to package directions. Stir in remaining ingredients. Drop by spoonfuls on a greased cookie sheet. Chill and eat.

Patricia Henderson, Mountaineers Alumni

Candy and Cookie Bark

4 (3-ounce) bars mint chocolate, broken in pieces
3 (100-calorie) packets Oreo Thin Crisps, coarsely crumbled, divided
3 medium-size peppermint candy canes, coarsely crushed

Line a baking sheet with foil. Melt chocolate in microwave on high stirring every 10 to 15 seconds, or in a saucepan over very low heat, stirring often until smooth. Stir in 1 cup crumbled cookies. Scrape onto a lined cookie sheet. Spread to about ¼-inch thick. Immediately sprinkle with crushed candy canes and remaining crumbled cookies. Pat in slightly. Refrigerate until firm, about 45 minutes. Cut in uneven pieces. Refrigerate airtight with wax paper between layers. The recipe makes about a pound or 24 pieces.

Variations: 1. Use a 12-ounce bag of white chocolate chips instead of mint chocolate bars. 2. Spoon chocolate mixture into decorative paper candy cups instead of onto a baking sheet. 3. Substitute 1¼ cups chopped nuts for the cookies and chopped crystallized ginger for the candy canes.

Bill Lilly, Lilly and Line Families,
Jumping Branch

Fantasy Fudge

Mom often made fudge when we were growing up, using a candy thermometer or a drop of candy in cold water testing to see if it was done. I never got the hang of it. Sometimes she didn't either and we ate the delicious "spoon candy." Around 1976, my friend and neighbor Anita E., showed me how to make this version of no-fail fudge and a new holiday tradition was born in my house, my mother's house, my mother-in-law's house, and many friends' houses.

3 cups sugar
¾ cup margarine or butter
1 (5-ounce) can evaporated milk
1 (12-ounce) bag semisweet chocolate chips
1 teaspoon vanilla extract
1 (10-ounce) jar marshmallow cream
1 cup chopped walnuts, optional

Have all ingredients measured and lined up on the counter. Once base cooks, everything goes very quickly. Prepare a 9x13-inch pan by lining it with aluminum foil, allowing foil to overlap sides to use as handles later. If you don't want to use foil, butter the pan. Combine sugar, margarine and evaporated milk in a large heavy saucepan or Dutch oven. Bring to a full, rolling boil over medium heat while stirring constantly. Continue boiling 5 minutes over medium heat while stirring. Remove from heat. Quickly add chocolate chips and stir until melted. Add vanilla extract, marshmallow cream and nuts. Beat until well blended. You have to be quick, but thorough. Under beating the fudge yields a grainy texture, but it will still be delicious. Pour into prepared pan and smooth top. Cool to room temperature. Makes 3 pounds.

Fran Miller, Parkersburg

Potato Candy Pinwheels

½ cup leftover mashed potatoes
1 teaspoon vanilla
¼ teaspoon salt
4 to 5 cups powdered sugar
4 tablespoons peanut butter,
    softened

I've made this from scratch for several years from my mom's recipe, which was never really written down. As we grew older, and our waistlines grew bigger, we've limited making this sweet candy to only a few times a year.

Combine mashed potatoes, vanilla and salt in a bowl. Add powdered sugar 1 cup at a time, mixing with your hands or spoon until thick. You want a firm dough that will hold its shape. Divide mixture in half if needed to make your work easier. Place on a smooth surface sprinkled with powdered sugar. Roll evenly into a rectangle about ½ inch thick, spread with peanut butter and gently roll up like a jelly roll. Wrap in plastic wrap and chill to set. Remove wrap and slice into pinwheel pieces to serve.

Barney Gullatt, West Virginia Mountaineers

Candied Apples

2 cups water
1 cup sugar
⅓ cup red cinnamon candies
6 large cooking apples, cored,
    peeled and quartered

This recipe is a simple and delicious one that Bill Lilly says is a specialty of Sarah Lilly Chapman and Robert "Bear Wallow Bob" Lilly. Bill's good friend, Carolyn McMahen, says that Bill has two fun sayings that he and other family members like to say. First, "If you're not a Lilly, you want to be, or should be, a Lilly!" And second, because the Lilly family has grown so much, "So glad we all came from Adam and Eve LILLY!"

Combine water, sugar and cinnamon candies in large saucepan. Cook over medium-high heat until candies are melted. Lower heat and cook 10 minutes longer. Add apples to syrup. Cook over low heat until syrup has cooked down and apples are tender but not mushy. Serve warm or cold.

Bill Lilly, Lilly and Line Families,
Jumping Branch

Clay County
Golden Delicious Festival

Clay
Third Week in September

The Clay County Golden Delicious Festival features four days of music and entertainment, crafts, parade, games and rides, pageants, quilt show, motorcycle show, antique car show, golf tournament and an outdoor drama. You will also discover, of course, baking contests with lots of food all brought together to celebrate the Golden Delicious Apple that was discovered on the Mullins Farm in Clay County.

304-587-4260
www.claygoldendeliciousfestival.com

Caramel Chocolate Chip Apples

Use Golden Delicious apples from West Virginia or smaller sweet red apples.

1 pound caramels
2 tablespoons water
Small dash salt
6 wooden skewers
6 medium-size apples
Chopped nuts
Chocolate chips

Melt caramels with water in double boiler, stirring frequently until smooth. Add salt. Place each apple on a countertop and steady it with your fingers. Do not hold apple in your hand when inserting skewer or it could go too far and end up sticking your hand. Press a skewer into end but do not push all the way through. Dip each apple in caramel syrup and turn to coat. Remove from caramel and quickly roll in chopped nuts and chocolate chips. Work fast and if caramel gets too thick add a few drops of water. Place each apple on wax paper to set. You can chill in the fridge as well.

Kimmie Morgan, West Virginia

Wilma Jones' Ginger Candy

Martha Sparks shared this wonderful recipe and story with her readers about a ginger candy once made by Wilma Dempsey Jones, a 15-year breast cancer survivor. According to Sparks, before Jones began chemotherapy, she tried to find ginger candy because she knew ginger helped in dealing with nausea. When she could not find any she decided to make her own. Because it helped her with her own nausea, she made additional batches for other cancer patients.

Jones lost her battle with breast cancer in 2008, but she is remembered for her dedication to helping others who suffered from the effects of chemotherapy and other medications or illnesses that caused nausea.

Over the years the candy and its recipe have been sent all over the U.S. and to other countries. (Note: Ginger may interfere with blood clotting and should be used by cancer or surgery patients only after talking to their doctors.)

2 tablespoons powdered ginger
2 cups Domino pure sugar
⅔ cup light corn syrup
½ cup water
Powdered sugar

Generously coat a baking sheet with powdered sugar and set aside. Using a wooden spoon, stir first 4 ingredients in a saucepan over low heat until dissolved. Increase heat to high. Bring mixture to a boil without stirring and cook 15 to 20 minutes to hard-crack stage (300° on a candy thermometer). If you don't have a candy thermometer, test by dropping a small amount into a glass of very cold water. If hard, brittle threads form it is ready. Remove from heat, taking care in handling the hot liquid. Quickly pour onto baking sheet in a thin stream. Cool at room temperature and break into small pieces. Coat with powdered sugar.

Wilma Dempsey Jones, The Jones Family, and Martha Sparks, the Logan Banner, Logan

Mountain Rock Candy

1½ cups water
6 cups sugar, divided
Liquid food coloring
Candy flavoring, optional
3 (6-inch) pieces string

My West Virginia mom grew up making and eating rock candy. When I was a little girl, we would make this treat anytime we had a surplus of sugar. Our only addition was food coloring. When my mom, now a grandmother, helped her grandchildren make it, she started using candy flavoring which was not readily available "back in the day."

Bring water to boil in a saucepan. Remove from heat and add 3 cups sugar, stirring until dissolved. Slowly add remaining sugar, reheating water if necessary. When all sugar is dissolved, pour mixture into 3 heat-proof jars or glasses. Stir 3 drops liquid food coloring and ½ teaspoon candy flavoring into each jar. Tie each length of string around a pencil. Lay a pencil on top of each jar so strings hang down into liquid. Crystals will begin to form in 1 hour, and continue to solidify for several days. If a layer forms on the surface of the jar, break it. When liquid completely evaporates, candy is ready.

Patricia Henderson, Mountaineers Alumni

Cranny Crow Overlook
at Lost River State Park near Mathias

West Virginia Honey Brittle

2 cups sugar
1 cup West Virginia honey
1 cup water

1 tablespoon butter
2 cups salted peanuts

Put sugar, honey and water in saucepan. Stir until sugar is dissolved. Heat to 300° on a candy thermometer. Remove from heat. Add butter and peanuts. Stir just enough to mix thoroughly. Pour in very thin sheets onto a well-greased platter. Cool. Break into pieces to serve.

M.C. Aldridge, WVU

Uniquely West Virginia Wine and Food Festival

Berkeley Springs
April

Uniquely West Virginia Wind and Food Festival includes more than a score of West Virginia wineries and edible product makers and growers set up for a daylong sampling and sale of their products. All weekend long, local restaurants and shops join in with related specials and sales. The show offers a free opportunity for the public to sample and buy dozens of state-grown products as well as meet the faces behind these products.

304-258-9147
www.berkeleysprings.com/newtbs/
uniquely-west-virginia-wine-food-festival

Orange Juice Taffy

2 cups sugar
¼ cup water
½ cup orange juice

Combine ingredients in saucepan. Cook until a drop forms very hard-ball stage (265° on a candy thermometer), stirring only until sugar dissolves. Pour into greased shallow pan. When cool enough to handle, pull until light. Cut with scissors or cool and break in pieces. Makes 2 dozen pieces.

Ginny Covington, Marshall

Candied Orange Peel

4 large oranges, tops and bottoms cut off
4 cups sugar, divided
3 cups water

Cut peel of each orange into 4 vertical segments and remove from orange. Cut into strips. Cook in large pot of boiling water 15 minutes; drain, rinse and drain again. Bring 3 cups sugar and 3 cups water to boil in medium saucepan over medium heat, stirring until sugar is dissolved. Add peel. Return to boil. Reduce heat; simmer 45 minutes. Drain. Toss peel and 1 cup sugar on rimmed baking sheet, separating strips. Lift peel from sugar and transfer to sheet of foil. Let stand until coating is dry, 1 to 2 days. Makes 3 cups.

Cinnamon Sugared Walnuts or Pecans

½ cup sugar
2 tablespoons ground cinnamon
4 cups walnut or pecan halves
1 egg white

In the early 1980's, I received a small tin of these delicious nuts and my holiday gifting changed forever. After begging the recipe from the mother of the student who gave them to me, I have made and shared these every Christmas since. It's easy to make a double batch; your family and friends will be glad you did.

Preheat oven to 300°. In a small bowl, mix sugar and cinnamon together. Set aside. Put nuts in a medium bowl and mix in egg white. Stir together until all nuts are coated. Pour sugar-cinnamon mixture over nuts and stir together well. Spread nuts on a rimmed cookie sheet in a single layer. Bake at 300° for 25 to 30 minutes, or until nuts are toasted and dry. Check early the first time you make them in case your oven is running a little hot. You don't want to over bake them. Serve warm or cool completely. Store in an airtight container. Put out some to share while you stash the ones intended as gifts. Save some back just for you.

Fran Miller, Parkersburg

PIES & OTHER DESSERTS

West Virginia Apple Crunch, page 227

Mixed Berry Pie

3 cups mixed berries
1 (8-inch) double pie crust
¾ to 1 cup West Virginia honey depending on sweetness of fruit
2 tablespoons cornstarch or 4 tablespoons flour
½ teaspoon cinnamon
1 tablespoon butter

Pick over and wash berries. Place in pastry-lined 8-inch pie pan. Add a little honey to cornstarch. Blend well. Add remainder of honey. Pour over berries. Sprinkle with cinnamon and bits of butter. Cover with crisscross pastry. Bake in preheated 450° oven 10 minutes. Reduce heat to 350° and bake 30 minutes.

M.C. Aldridge, WVU

Nick's Blackberry Pie

4 cups blackberries
4 tablespoons tapioca
1½ cups sugar

2 teaspoons vanilla extract
2 pie crusts for an 8-inch pie

Mix berries in a large bowl with tapioca, sugar and vanilla. Set aside for 15 minutes, more if berries are frozen. Pour berries into pie crust. Top with second crust. Pinch edges together to seal and cut vent slits in top crust. Bake in preheated 400° oven 45 to 50 minutes. Use a drip pan such as a cookie sheet to catch drippings or get ready to clean your oven. Let pie cool before serving.

Nick Durm, Beckley

Blackberry Pie

1 (15-ounce) package pastry
    for a 9-inch double crust pie
4 cups fresh blackberries
1½ cups sugar

½ cup all-purpose flour
¼ teaspoon salt
1 tablespoon butter

Preheat oven to 325°. Line a 9-inch, deep-dish pie pan with 1 crust. Place blackberries in a large bowl. Stir together sugar, flour and salt. Sprinkle over berries and toss to coat. Pour into pie crust. Dot with butter. Place second pie crust over top and seal edges by pressing with a fork or fluting with your fingers. Cut a design in top crust with a sharp knife to vent steam. Bake 1 hour or until top crust is browned. Let cool to almost room temperature before serving to allow filling to set.

West Virginia Blackberry Festival

Nutter Fort
First Weekend in August

West Virginia Blackberry Festival is a family festival with free admission, free parking, and free quality entertainment, West Virginia Blackberry Festival has food, novelty, craft, and snack vendors on site, as well as amusement rides, bounces, climbing wall, and more. Live musical entertainment takes place on a professional stage.

Other events include a car parade, pet parade, baking contest, talent contest, and a 5K run.

304-709-3206 • www.wvblackberry.com

Apple Butter Pumpkin Pie

1 cup canned pumpkin purée
1 cup apple butter
¼ cup dark brown sugar
½ teaspoon ground cinnamon
½ teaspoon ground nutmeg

¼ teaspoon salt
3 eggs, beaten
1 cup evaporated milk
1 (9-inch) unbaked deep-dish pie
  crust

STREUSEL TOPPING:

3 tablespoons butter, softened
½ cup all-purpose flour

⅓ cup dark brown sugar
½ cup chopped pecans

Preheat oven to 350°. In a large bowl, combine pumpkin, apple butter, brown sugar, cinnamon, nutmeg and salt. Stir in eggs and evaporated milk. Pour into prepared pie shell. Bake 50 to 60 minutes or until set. While pie is baking, make the topping. Combine butter, flour and brown sugar in a small bowl. Stir until mixture resembles coarse crumbs. Stir in pecans. When pie is set, sprinkle Streusel Topping over top, and bake an additional 15 minutes.

Key Lime Pie

1 (8-inch) pie crust
5 egg yolks
2 (14-ounce) cans sweetened condensed milk
1 cup lime juice

Partially bake pie crust at 325° for 5 minutes. Do not overcook or allow to brown. Mix remaining ingredients in large bowl and spoon into partially baked crust. Bake in 325° oven 20 minutes.

Nick Durm, Beckley

Lemon Cake Pie

2 eggs, separated
1 unbaked 8-inch pie crust
1 cup sugar
¼ cup flour
¼ cup melted margarine or butter
⅛ teaspoon salt
1 lemon, its juice and grated peel
1 cup milk

This recipe was handed down from my great-grandmother Emma Bowles Toney, to my grandmother, and to my mother, and I share it in memory of them all. When cut, there will be a delicate cake on top of the pie mixture.

Beat egg whites until stiff but not dry. Set aside. Bake pie shell at 350° for only 5 minutes and set aside. Combine sugar, flour, margarine, salt and egg yolks in mixer bowl. Beat until smooth. Beat in lemon juice and lemon peel. Add milk, beating slowly. Fold, not beat, egg whites into lemon mixture. Pour filling into baked pie shell and bake 40 minutes or until filling is firm.

Brenda Beatty,
St. Albans Historical Society, St. Albans

Pawpaw Chiffon Pie

I've been working with pawpaws for more than 30 years, since working on my Masters in Plant Genetics at West Virginia State University. I tasted my first pawpaw in 1975 and since have studied the plants and their history extensively. The Lewis and Clark Expedition ate them on their return trip through Missouri when their rations and game ran low, early settlers dined on them, and there are cities and towns named after them in West Virginia, Kentucky, Michigan, and Oklahoma. The fruit, sometimes called a West Virginia banana (or Indiana banana, Michigan banana, etc.) is best eaten raw if you want to savor its complex and exquisite flavor. But, if you want to try a few recipes using pawpaw as an ingredient, pies and ice cream are a good fit. You could use a peach ice cream recipe and substitute pawpaw purée for the peach. This wonderful pie recipe is from Marilyn Kluger's 1973 book, The Wild Flavor. *You can use a regular pie crust or a graham cracker crust if you desire.*

1½ tablespoons gelatin
¼ cup cold water
½ cup sugar, granulated or brown
½ teaspoon salt
3 egg yolks, beaten
½ cup milk

1 cup puréed pawpaw pulp
3 egg whites
¼ cup granulated sugar
1 cup heavy cream, whipped, divided
1 baked 9-inch pastry shell

Soften gelatin in cold water. Combine ½ cup sugar with salt, egg yolks and milk in top of a double boiler. Cook over boiling water, stirring constantly, until mixture coats a spoon. Remove from heat and stir in softened gelatin and pawpaw purée. Chill until a spoonful holds its shape, about half an hour. Beat egg whites stiff with ¼ cup granulated sugar. Fold egg whites and half the whipped cream into filling. Pour into pastry shell. Spread remaining whipped cream on top of pie.

Neal Peterson, Peterson Pawpaws,
Harpers Ferry

Coconut Custard Impossible Icebox Pie

2 cups milk
½ cup Bisquick baking mix
¾ cup sugar
4 eggs
4 tablespoons (½ stick) butter
    or margarine
1½ teaspoons vanilla extract
1 cup flaked coconut

This recipe has been around for decades and is a family favorite, especially in the summer. The Bisquick settles to the bottom to make a crust of sorts, making it firm enough to serve up to waiting diners. Here's my trick: Mix it up in the blender, then pour it into a pie dish. That makes it good and quick. What's so "impossible" about that?

Preheat oven to 350°. Spray an 8-inch deep-dish pie plate with cooking spray. Set aside. Measure milk in blender container, and add all ingredients except coconut. Blend for 3 minutes on low speed. Pour mixture into prepared pie plate. Let set for 5 minutes. Sprinkle evenly with coconut. Bake 35 to 40 minutes, until pie is set and coconut is golden brown. Cool 30 minutes and then refrigerate until chilled before serving. Refrigerate any leftovers. As if!

Fran Miller, Parkersburg

Banana Chocolate Cream Pie

1 (8-inch) deep-dish pie shell
1 banana
1 (3.4-ounce) package vanilla instant pudding mix
1½ cups milk
1 (8-ounce) container whipped topping, plus more for topping
   if desired
Chocolate chips or chocolate hard-shell coating

Bake pie shell as directed on package. You may want to add some slits to keep bubbles from popping up. While pie shell is baking, peel and slice banana. Remove pie shell from oven and place aside to cool. Mix pudding mix and milk; stir in whipped topping. Place bananas on bottom of pie shell and cover with filling. If you are using chocolate chips sprinkle them over top. Chill in refrigerator about an hour before serving, topped with additional whipped topping if desired. If you are using hard-shell coating, add it just before you serve pie. Allow coating to harden and then top with additional whipped topping if desired.

C.L. Feinstein, WVU

Tabler Family Raspberry Cobbler

This cobbler recipe by my mom, Pat Tabler, was, and still is, a family standard in July. My grandparents told of going into the woods to pick berries when they were kids, and that tradition carried down to my generation. I cherish the tradition now. However, as a young teen I loved the cobbler but hated wearing jeans, boots, and long-sleeved sweatshirts in the withering humidity of July in West Virginia. The clothes helped protect us in case of snake bites. We always came back from the woods drenched in sweat with our hands scratched to smithereens.

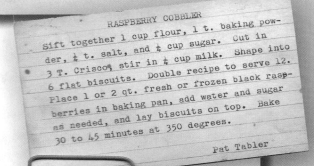

1 cup flour
1 teaspoon baking powder
¼ teaspoon salt
¼ cup sugar
3 tablespoons Crisco
¼ cup milk
1 to 2 quarts black raspberries
Water
Sugar as needed

Sift together 1 cup flour, 1 teaspoon baking powder, ¼ teaspoon salt and ¼ cup sugar. Cut in 3 tablespoons Crisco, stir in ¼ cup milk. Shape into flat biscuits. Double recipe to serve 12. Place 1 or 2 quarts fresh or frozen black raspberries in baking pan, add water and sugar as needed, and lay biscuits on top. Bake 30 to 45 minutes at 350°. —Pat Tabler

Note from Kent: The directions are taken directly from Pat Tabler's recipe card in order to keep it in her own voice.

Dave Tabler and Family, Martinsburg

Simple Strawberry Tarts

6 wonton wrappers
2 tablespoons sugar-free jelly or fruit spread
1½ cups diced fresh strawberries
3 ounces (6 tablespoons) fat-free yogurt

Use any flavor jelly and yogurt, and any type of fresh fruit you prefer.

Preheat oven to 375°. Press wonton wrappers into muffin tins, allowing corners to stand up over edges. Bake wontons until lightly browned, about 5 minutes. Watch carefully, they brown very quickly. Remove from oven, let cool and carefully remove each wonton shell from muffin pan. Warm jelly in microwave 7 to 10 seconds. Lightly coat insides of each shell with melted jelly. Fill with ¼ cup fruit and top with 1 tablespoon yogurt.

West Virginia University Extension Service,
Morgantown, www.ext.wvu.edu

West Virginia Strawberry Festival

Buckhannon
Third Week in May

The West Virginia Strawberry Festival began in 1936 as a one-day event to honor local strawberry farmers. Now 73+ years later, the event is a week of community fun with tasty strawberry treats, a carnival, arts and craft shows, musical performances and more. Join us for a week of fun for the whole family.

304-472-9036
www.WVStrawberryFestival.com

West Virginia Apple Crunch

Johnny Appleseed, whose real name was Johnny Chapman, visited the Wellsburg, West Virginia area in the early 1800's and planted several apple orchards. Johnny Chapman grew into a legendary figure as he traveled the country as a planter, apple expert, nursery developer, and preacher. As the nurseries developed, apple trees were distributed throughout the area. The West Virginia Grimes Golden Apple, developed by Thomas Grimes around 1805, is said to have come from a tree planted by Johnny "Appleseed" Chapman. According to Frank Chapman, the great-great-grandson of Johnny Appleseed's half-brother, Nathaniel, the Grimes Golden apple tree was probably planted by Grimes from a seedling or seed provided by Johnny Appleseed, noting that Johnny Appleseed preferred planting nurseries. "It was Johnny's habit to plant nurseries, not one or even a few trees." The Golden Delicious apple, which was discovered by Anderson Mullins in Clay County West Virginia in 1905, was designated the official state fruit by the West Virginia State Legislature on February 20, 1995. Before then, the official state fruit was simply the plain apple.

Vegetable spray
8 medium apples, cored and
   sliced thin
½ cup raisins, optional
⅓ cup flour
1 teaspoon cinnamon
1 cup rolled oats
⅓ cup packed brown sugar
¼ cup margarine
½ cup chopped walnuts, optional

Spray pan 8-inch square pan with vegetable spray. Place apples and raisins in baking pan. In mixing bowl combine flour, cinnamon, oats and sugar. Cut in margarine using a pastry blender or 2 knives. Stir in walnuts. Sprinkle flour-oat mixture over apples. Bake at 350° for 35 to 40 minutes. Makes 8 servings.

Variation: To make a Peach Crisp, substitute 6 cups canned drained or fresh peaches for the apples.

West Virginia University Extension Service,
Morgantown, www.ext.wvu.edu

Easy Baked Apple Cinnamon Crisps

West Virginia is the home of the Golden Delicious apple. We made these tasty treats every year in the fall. For a treat, serve hot with a scoop of vanilla ice cream.

4 apples, cored
2 to 3 teaspoons sugar
4 to 5 teaspoons cinnamon

Preheat oven to 225°. Slice apples into thin, chip-size pieces. Mix sugar and cinnamon in a bowl and toss apple chips to coat, making sure all sides are coated. Place apple chips in a single layer on cookie sheets lined with parchment paper. Bake 1 hour, turn them over and bake another hour. Turn oven off and let them cool in oven. If you want to serve hot with ice cream, remove from oven after first hour and serve as quickly as possible. They will still be a bit mushy and perfect for topping with ice cream.

Hannah B. Turner, West Virginia

Burlington Old-Fashioned Apple Harvest Festival

Burlington
First Full Weekend in October

Burlington Old-Fashioned Apple Harvest Festival is a free two-day event including live entertainment, a Banjo & Fiddle contest, a baby apple dumpling contest, parade, and, of course, old-fashioned apple butter and apple dumplings. There are many food and craft vendors on site as well as a car show and fireworks on the last night. This is a great event for the whole family.

800-969-0079 • www.bumfs.org

Baked Apples

West Virginia apples (how many you want to make)

PER APPLE:

2 tablespoons granulated sugar

4 teaspoons margarine, softened

¼ cup raisins

1 tablespoon flour

⅓ cup firmly packed brown sugar

½ teaspoon cinnamon

1 tablespoon water

Preheat oven to 350°. Treat a glass baking dish with nonstick spray. Core apples, all the way through, and peel away skin from around tops. Slice away a small piece from bottom of each apple so they will stand up straight in dish. Place apples in dish. Mix together granulated sugar and margarine with raisins and place in cored out cavity of each apple. Bake approximately 20 minutes. Meanwhile in a small bowl, combine flour, brown sugar and cinnamon along with water. Spoon over baking apples and continue to bake another 10 minutes. Serve either warm or cool.

The Honorable & Mrs. John D. Rockefeller IV,
United States Senator, West Virginia

Susan's Baklava

1 (16-ounce) package filo dough, thawed
½ pound butter, melted
½ pound walnuts, finely ground
½ pound almonds, finely ground
2 cups sugar, divided
½ cup honey
½ cup water
½ medium lemon, cut in slices

Butter a 9x13-inch baking pan. Place 4 sheets of filo dough in pan, sprinkling each with butter before adding next sheet. Combine ground nuts and 1 cup sugar. Sprinkle 4 tablespoons on top of filo layers. Continue layering with 4 sheets filo sprinkled with butter and topped with 4 tablespoons nut mixture, ending with filo layers. Do not butter top layer. Press firmly but carefully to adhere all layers. Very carefully cut filo layers into diamond-shaped pieces, cutting each way from corner to corner in pan. Dribble last of butter over top. Bake in 300° oven 45 minutes or until golden brown. Meanwhile, prepare syrup. Boil together honey, 1 cup sugar, water and lemon slices until thickened, about 20 minutes. Remove lemon. Pour warm syrup over baklava as soon as it is removed from oven. Cool. Makes 32 servings.

Steve Cotton, Voice of the Thundering Herd,
Marshall University, Huntington

Grandma Hallie's Custard

Grandma Hallie was a true "Depression cook." She was an 18-year-old wife and her son was born six weeks before the 1929 Stock Market Crash. They had to move back to the family farm to survive. Making custard was the "old" way to use up extra eggs and milk before there was refrigeration. Honey or molasses was used as sweeteners; vanilla was used only if available. Folks "made do." This dessert was my late father's favorite. Here's to my dad and grandma. I miss them every day.

4 large eggs
2½ cups milk
½ cup sugar
1 teaspoon vanilla extract
½ teaspoon salt
Ground nutmeg, optional

Preheat oven to 350°. In a medium bowl, mix eggs, milk, sugar, vanilla and salt with an eggbeater or a mixer on low speed until evenly blended. Pour into an ungreased 8x8-inch casserole dish. Sprinkle with nutmeg, if desired. Set casserole dish into a 9x13-inch pan. Place pans in oven and carefully pour hot water into larger pan to a depth of 1 inch, taking care to not getting any water into custard. Bake 45 minutes and test for doneness by slipping a knife blade into center of custard. If it comes out pretty clean, remove pans from oven. Remove casserole dish from water bath to stop the cooking. Do not over bake. Cool, and then refrigerate until ready to eat. (OK, I admit that I like mine warm.)

Variation: This custard can also be baked in individual ramekins. Fill 6 ramekins with custard and place in oven in water bath as described above. Bake at 325° (note lower temperature) 20 to 30 minutes, using knife test to check for doneness.

Fran Miller, Parkersburg

Nelson Family Bread Pudding

2 cups milk
4 cups dry bread, torn in pieces
¼ cup melted butter
½ cup sugar
2 eggs, slightly beaten
¼ teaspoon salt
½ cup seeded raisins
1 teaspoon cinnamon, optional
Strawberries and whipped cream
  for topping

Heat oven to 350°. Butter a 1½-quart casserole dish and set aside. Heat milk to scalding and pour over bread. Lightly mix and allow to cool. Add remaining ingredients except toppings, stir well and pour into casserole dish. Bake at 350° for 40 to 50 minutes or until knife inserted into center comes out clean. Serve warm.

Candace Nelson, Morgantown, www.candacerosenelson.com

Lemon Fluff

2 (14.5-ounce) cans evaporated
  milk
1 (3-ounce) box lemon Jell-O
1¾ cups hot water
¼ cup lemon juice
1 cup sugar
2½ cups vanilla wafer crumbs,
  divided
Maraschino cherries

Chill unopened cans of evaporated milk until icy cold, at least 3 or 4 hours. Dissolve Jell-O in hot water; chill until partially set. Whip until light and fluffy. Add lemon juice and sugar. Whip chilled milk and fold into Jell-O mixture. Line bottom of 9x13-inch pan with 2 cups crumbs. Pour in lemon mixture. Top with remaining crumbs. Chill until firm. Cut into squares and place a maraschino cherry in the center of each piece. Serves 12.

Margaret Larew Moore,
St. Albans Historical Society, St. Albans

Easy Peach Dessert

White or yellow cake mix, plus
    ingredients to prepare per
    directions
3 fresh ripe peaches, sliced
½ to 1 cup brown sugar
1 stick butter, melted

Mix cake batter according to package directions. Put melted butter in a 9x13-inch baking dish; cover bottom with brown sugar. Layer sliced peaches over brown sugar and cover with cake mix. Bake according to package directions.

Eva Ansel
West Virginia Peach Festival

West Virginia Peach Festival

Romney
Second Weekend in August

The mission of West Virginia Peach Festival is to celebrate the growing of peaches in Hampshire County as well as the state of West Virginia. The state commissioner of agriculture crowns our king and queen, who win the position by writing an essay about agriculture in the area. We also have a Little Peach Fuzz and Peach Blossom, which are part of the royalty. The festival includes a myriad of activities geared around peaches including a hat contest, pie and peach eating contests, games, activities, live entertainment and artisans. The majority of the events are held at the historic Taggart Hall in Romney.

304-788-0903
www.facebook.com/pages/
West-Virginia-Peach-Festival

Apple Peach Bake

6 medium baking apples
¼ cup peach preserves
¼ teaspoon cinnamon
¼ cup apple cider or apple juice
¾ cup crumbled chewy oatmeal cookies

Cut apples in half and core. Place in 9x13-inch baking pan, cut side up. Combine preserves, cinnamon and apple cider. Drizzle over cut side of apples. Cover pan tightly with foil. Bake at 350° about 35 minutes or until apples are just tender. Sprinkle crumbled cookies over cut surface of apples and drizzle with preserve mixture from bottom of pan. Bake 5 minutes longer, uncovered. Serve warm or cold. Can be topped with whipped topping or frozen vanilla yogurt, if desired. Makes 6 servings.

Linda McKay, West Virginia

WEST VIRGINIA FESTIVALS

The following is a list of annual festivals found throughout the Mountain State. Chances are, we've neglected to include some events. If you aware of any we missed, call us toll-free 1.888.854.5954, and we'll do our best to include it in a subsequent printing. Keep in mind, too, that dates and venues change. Please verify all information before making plans to attend any of these events. Festivals are listed by month, then alphabetically by the city where the festival is held. Please call the number listed or visit the festival's website for more information.

JANUARY

Greenbrier
WV Shanghai Parade • 304-647-8024

FEBRUARY

Braxton
WV Sweetheart Festival • 304-765-3395
www.wvsweeheartpageant.com

Kanawha
Winterfest • 855-855-3378
www.saintalbansriverfest.com

MARCH

Pickens
West Virginia Maple Syrup Festival • 304-924-5363
www.pickenswv.squarespace.com/maple-syrup-festival

Ripley
WV Chocolate Festival • 304-372-3482

APRIL

Berkeley Springs
Uniquely West Virginia Wine and Food Festival
800-448-8797 • www.berkeleysprings.com/
uniquely-west-virginia-wine-food-festival-plus-
redbud-weekend

Buckeye
Wild Edibles Festival • 304-799-4636
www.pocahontascountywv.com

Elkins
Ramps & Rail Festival • 304-635-7803
www.mountainrailwv.com

Grant
Spring Mountain Festival • 304-257-2722
www.gowv.com

Lewis
WV Cattleman's Beef Expo • 304-472-4020
www.wvbeef.org

Lewisburg
Lewisburg Chocolate Festival • 304-645-1000
www.lewisburgchocolatefestival.com

Martinsburg
Martinsburg Chocolate Festival • 304–262–4200
www.mainstreetmartinsburg.com

MAY

Clay
Elk River Pedal & Paddle Challenge • 304-587-4455
www.elkriverpedalandpaddle.com

Buckhannon
WV Strawberry Festival • 304-472-9036
www.wvstrawberryfestival.com

Greenbrier
WV Dandelion Festival • 304-536-5060
www.wssmainstreet.org

WV Veterans Reunion • 304-445-4047
www.4seasonspageant.com

Harrison
Scottish Festival & Celtic Gathering • 304-534-3737
www.scots-westvirginia.org

Lost City
Fiber Fest • Lost River Education Foundation
304-897-7242

MAY (cont.)

Mercer
Cole Chevy Mountain Festival • 304-327-7184
www.bluefieldchamber.com

Marion
Lower West Fork River Fest • 304-287-2880

WV Three Rivers Festival • 304-366-2625
www.wvthreeriversfestival.org

Pendleton
Springfest • 304-358-3884
www.pendletoncounty.com

Webster
Webster County Woodchopping Festival
304-847-7666
www.webstercountywoodchopping.com

JUNE

Boone
WV Coal Festival • 304-369-3391

Braxton
WV Timber & Wood Products Show • 304-372-1955
www.wvfa.org

Calhoun
Calhoun County Wood Festival • 304-531-0084
www.calhounwoodfest.com

Fayette
New River Gorge Heritage Festival • 304-574-1668
www.townoffayetteville.org

White Oak Rail Trail Expo • 304-573-1165

Gilmer
WV State Folk Festival • 304-462-8900
www.wvstatefolkfestival.com

Greenbrier
Badlands Bluegrass Festival • 781-771-4275
www.badlandsbluegrass.com

Ronceverte River Festival • 304-647-3825

Hampshire
Romney History Festival • 304-822-5118

Jefferson
Mountain Heritage Arts & Crafts Festival
304-725-2055
www.jeffersoncountywvchamber.org

Kanawha
FestivAll Charleston • 304-470-0489
www.festivallcharleston.com

Saint Albans Riverfest • 855-855-3378
www.saintalbansriverfest.com

Mason
Point Pleasant Sternwheel Regatta • 304-593-2404
www.pointpleasantregatta.org

Pocahontas
Little Levels Heritage Fair • 304-653-4897
www.littlelevelsheritagefair.com

Preston
WV Miniature Horse Championship • 304-783-4827

Wood
Mid Ohio Valley Multi Cultural Festival
304-482-7790 • www.movmcf.org

JULY

Braxton
Braxton's Mountain Lakes Festival • 304-765-6533
www.mountainlakesfestival.com

Cabell
Cabell County Fair • 304-743-6970
www.cabellcountyfair.org

Hurricane 4th of July Celebration • 304-562-5896
www.hurricanewv.com

Greenbrier
Alderson 4th of July Celebration • 304-445-7730

Hardy
WV Poultry Convention & Festival • 304-530-2725

Harrison
Bridgeport Benedum Festival • 304-842-8240
www.bridgeport.com/parksandrec

Huntington
WV Hot Dog Festival • 304-525-7788
www.WVHotDogFestival.com

Jackson
Jackson County Jr. Fair • 304-372-5066 • wwwjcjf.net

Mountain State Art & Craft Fair • 304-372-3247
www.msacf.com

Ripley 4th of July Celebration • 304-531-3571

Lewis
Lewis County Fair • 304-472-5303
www.lewiscountyfair.com

Logan
WV Freedom Festival • 304-752-3036
www.facebook.com/wvfreedomfestival

Marion
Paw Paw District Fair • 304-278-7042
www.pawpawfairgrounds.com

Marlinton
WV Roadkill Cook-off • 800-336-7009
www.pccocwv.com

Marshall
Marshall County Fair • 304-845-8659
www.marshallcountyfair.net

Mineral
Mineral County Fair • 304-298-4566

Monongalia
Monongalia County Fair • 304-291-7201
www.moncountyfair.org

Nicholas
Cherry River Festival • 304-846-9114
www.cherryriverfestival.org

Nicholas County Fair • 304-872-1454

Nicholas County Kids Summerfest • 304-651-6047

Pocahontas
Pocahontas County Pioneer Days • 304-799-4452

Putnam
Putnam County Fair • 304-586-4001

Raleigh
Friends of Coal Auto Fair • 304-252-0715
www.friendsofcoalautofair.com

Summers
John Henry Days • 304-466-3745
www.johnhenryhistoricalpark.com

Webster
Cowen Historical Railroad Festival • 304-226-5682

Wetzel
Festival of Memories • 304-771-4551

AUGUST

Barbour
Barbour County Fair • 304-823-1328
www.barbourcountyfair.com

Berkeley
Berkeley County Youth Fair • 304-279-2581
www.berkeleycountyyouthfair.org

Bluefield
Lemonade Festival • 304-589-0239
www.bluefieldpreservationsociety.com

Charleston
Ribfest BBQ Festival • 304-444-2921
www.charlestonwvribfest.com

Clarksburg
WV Italian National Pasta Cookoff • 304-622-2157
www.wvihf.com

Doddridge
Doddridge County Fair • 304-873-1742
www.doddridgecountyfaincom

AUGUST (cont.)

Fairmont
Tomato Tasting Festival • 304-816-1379

Fayette
Meadow Bridge Homecoming Festival
304-484-7124
www.meadowbridgehomecomingfestival.com

Greenbrier
The State Fair of West Virginia • 304-645-1090
www.statefairofwv.com

Hampshire
Hampshire County Fair • 304-496-7272

Jefferson
Jefferson County Fair • 304-724-1411
www.jeffersoncountyfairwv.org

Kanawha
Pinch Reunion Festival • 304-541-9026
www.pinchreunion.webs.com

South Charleston Summerfest • 304-419-6197

Lincoln
Heat'n the Hills • 304-824-5806
www.heatnthehills.com

Marion
Mannington District Fair • 304-986-1911
www.manningtondistrictfair.org

Mason
Mason County Fair • 304-675-5463
www.masoncountyfairwvorg

Mercer
Mercer County Fair • 304-887-6716
www.fairofmercercounty.com

Monongalia
Clay District Fair • 304-798-3700

Nutter Fort
WV Blackberry Festival • 304-622-3206
www.wvblackberry.com

Parkersburg
West Virginia Honey Festival • 304-428-1130

Raleigh
Appalachian Festival • 304-252-7328
www.appalachianfestival.net

Randolph
Augusta Heritage Center Festival • 304-637-1245
www.augustaheritagecenter.org

Romney
West Virginia Peach Festival • 304-822-7477
www.cometohampshire.com

Snowshoe
Blues, Brews, & BBQ Festival • 304-572-5892
www.snowshoemtn.com

Taylor
Taylor County Fair • 304-265-4367

Tucker
Tucker County Fair • 304-642-0641
www.tuckercountyfair.com

Tyler
Tyler County Fair • 304-758-2349

Wetzel
Paden City Labor Day Celebration • 304-771-1574

Town & Country Days • 304-455-4275
www.townandcountrydays.org

Wirt
Wirt County Fair • 304-275-3101
www.wirtcofair.com

Wood
Parkersburg Homecoming Festival • 304-588-6245
www.parkersburg-homecoming.com

SEPTEMBER

Arnoldsburg
West Virginia Molasses Festival • 304-655-7371

Braxton
Burnsville Harvest Festival • 304-853-2605

Brooke
Brooke County Fair • 304-737-2863
www.brookecountyfair.org

Cabell
Barboursville Fall Festival • 304-736-9820
www.barboursville.org

Chapmanville
Chapmanville Apple Butter Festival • 304-688-3483

Clay
Clay County Golden Delicious Festival
304-587-7323
www.claygoldendeliciousfestival.com

Fayette
Gauley Bridge Town Celebration • 304-632-2505

Oak Leaf Festival • 800-927-0263
www.missoaldeaffestival.com

Hampshire
Capon Bridge Founder's Day Festival
304-856-1118 • www.cbfoundersdayfestival.com

Hancock
Hancock County Old Time Fair • 304-287-0298

Harrison
Frontier Days • 304-777-7748
www.shinnstonwv.com

Huntington
ChiliFest • 304-634-4857 • www.chilifestwv.com

Kanawha
Clendenin Fall Festival • 304-400-4029

Kingwood
Preston County Buckwheat Festival • 304-379-2203
www.buckwheatfest.com

Lincoln
WV Hillbilly Days • 304-549-7301
www.lcfairsandfestivals.com

Mercer
Princeton Autumnfest • 304-487-1502
www.pmccc.com

Monongalia
Florence Merow Mason Dixon Festival of WV
304-599-1309 • www.masondixonfestival.com

Moorefield
Heritage Weekend
Hardy County Tour & Crafts Association
304-530-0280

Nicholas
Craigsville Fall Festival • 681-355-0123

Pendleton
Treasure Mountain Festival • 304-358-3298
www.treasuremountainfestival.com

Pennsboro
Pennsboro Country Roads Festival • 304-299-0101
www.countryroadsfestival.com

Raleigh
Beckley's Kids Classic Festival • 304-256-1776
www.beckley.org

Randolph
Mountain State Forest Festival • 304-636-1824
www.forestfestival.com

Randolph County Fair • 304-642-7790
www.randolphcountyfairwv.com

Summersville
Kirkwood Winery Grape Stomping Wine Festival
304-872-7332 • www.kirkwood-wine.com

Nicholas County Potato Festival • 304-872-3722
www.nicholascountypotatofestival.com

Tyler
WV Oil & Gas Festival • 304-652-2939

Wood
Volcano Days • 304-679-3611
www.mountwoodpark.org

OCTOBER

Berkeley Springs
WV Apple Butter Festival • 304-258-3738
www.berkeleysprings.com/apple-butter-festival

Braxton
Sutton Fall Festival • 304-765-5581

Brooke
Christmas in the Park • 304-527-3378

Fairmont
Harvest Festival, Pricketts Fort State Park • 304-363-3030 • www.prickettsfort.org

Fayette
New River Gorge Bridge Day • 304-465-5617
www.officialbridgeday.con

Jackson
Ravenswood Octoberfest • 304-761-8480
www.ravenswoodoctoberfest.com

Kanawha
Charleston Blvd. Rod Run & Doo Wop •
304-941-6021 • www.charlestonwvcarshow.com

Keyser
Burlington Old Fashioned Apple Harvest Festival
304-289-6010 • www.bumfs.org/ahf.html

Lewisburg
Taste of Our Towns • 304-645-7917
www.carnegiehallwv.org

Manchester
Hogging Up BBQ Festival • 410-908-9241
www.hoggingup.com

Martinsburg
Main Street Martinsburg Chili Cook-Off
304-262-4200 • www.mainstreetmartinsburg.com

Mountain State Apple Harvest Festival
304-263-2500 • www.msahf.com

Mason
Battle Days of Point Pleasant • 304-593-6055
www.masoncounty.org

Mathias
WV Turkey Festival • 304-897-7282

Milton
WV Pumpkin Festival • 304-638-1633
www.wvpumpkinpark.com

Raleigh
Rocket Boys Festival • 540-580-3908
www.rocketboysfestival.com

Rowlesburg
West Virginia Chestnut Festival • 304-329-1240 •
www.wvchestnutfestival.com

Saint Albans
Morgan's Kitchen Fall Festival • 304-727-5972
www.stalbanshistory.com

Salem
Salem Apple Butter Festival • 304-782-3565
www.salemapplebutterfestival.com

Spencer
WV Black Walnut Festival • 304-927-5616
www.wvbwf.com .

Wayne
C-K AutumnFest, Inc. • 304-453-5420
www.ckautumnfest.com

Webster Springs
Burgoo Cook-off • 304- 847-7291
www.websterwv.com

Wetzel
Wetzel County Autumnfest • 304-775-2870
www.wetzelcoautumnfest.org

Wheeling
Ohio County Country Fair • 304-234-3673
www.ohiocountycountryfair.org

DECEMBER

Fairmont
Feast of the Seven Fishes Festival • 304-366-0468
www.mainstreetfairmont.org

INDEX

A

B

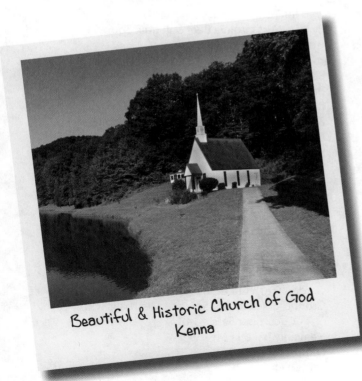

Beautiful & Historic Church of God
Kenna

West Virginia Maple Syrup Festival

More Great American Cookbooks

Eat & Explore Cookbook Series

Discover community celebrations and unique destinations, as they share their favorite recipes.

Explore the distinct flavor of each state by savoring 200 favorite local recipes. In addition, fun festivals, exciting events, unique attractions, and fascinating tourist destinations are profiled throughout the book with everything you need to plan your family's next getaway.

EACH: $18.95 • 256 pages • 8x9 • paperbound

Arkansas • Minnesota • North Carolina
Ohio • Oklahoma • Virginia • Washington

State Back Road Restaurants Series

Every Road Leads to Delicious Food.

From two-lane highways and interstates, to dirt roads and quaint downtowns, every road leads to delicious food when traveling across our United States. Each well-researched and charming guide leads you to the state's best back road restaurants. No time to travel? No problem. Each restaurant shares their favorite recipes—sometimes their signature dish, sometimes a family favorite, always delicious.

EACH: $18.95 • 256 pages • 7x9 • paperbound • full-color

Alabama • Kentucky • Tennessee • Texas

It's So Easy...

Kitchen Memories Cookbook

Your Recipe for Family Fun in the Kitchen

This kids' cookbook and free-style memory book guarantees hours of fun and a lifetime of memories for your family. It's a cookbook, a memory book, and an activity book—all in one! A cherished keepsake for your family.

Family Favorite Recipes

It's so easy to cook great food your family will love with 350 simply delicious recipes for easy-to-afford, easy-to-prepare dinners. It's so easy to encourage your family to eat more meals at home...to enjoy time spent in the kitchen... to save money making delicious affordable meals...to cook the foods your family loves without the fuss...with *Family Favorite Recipes*.

EACH: $18.95 • 248 to 256 pages • 7x10 • paperbound • full-color

www.GreatAmericanPublishers.com • www.facebook.com/GreatAmericanPublishers

State Hometown Cookbook Series

Each book features tried and true recipes that preserve the regional food traditions of the state—recipes for dishes that families have enjoyed over and over again. More than just cookbooks, the STATE HOMETOWN COOKBOOK SERIES is preserving your recipes for the next generation of hometown cooks.

Alabama • 978-1-934817-27-8

Georgia • 978-1-934817-01-8

Louisiana • 978-1-934817-07-0

Mississippi • 978-1-934817-08-7

South Carolina • 978-1-934817-10-0

Tennessee • 978-0-9779053-2-4

Texas • 978-1-934817-04-9

West Virginia • 978-1-934817-20-9

- Easy to follow recipes produce great-tasting dishes every time.
- Recipes use ingredients you already have in your pantry.
- Fun-to-read sidebars feature food-related festivals.
- The perfect gift or souvenir for anyone who loves to cook.

EACH: $18.95 • 240 to 272 pages • 8x9 • paperbound

Don't miss out on our upcoming titles—join our Cookbook Club and you'll be notified of each new edition.

www.GreatAmericanPublishers.com • www.facebook.com/GreatAmericanPublishers

---

Order Form MAIL TO: Great American Publishers • 171 Lone Pine Church Road • Lena, MS 39094
Or call us toll-free 1.888.854.5954 to order by check or credit card

❏ Check Enclosed
Charge to: ❏ Visa ❏ MC ❏ AmEx ❏ Disc

Card # _____

Exp Date Signature _____

Name_____

Address _____

City/State/Zip _____

Phone_____

Email_____

Qty.	Title	Total

Subtotal _____

Postage ($4 first book; $1 each additional) _____

Total _____